✪ WEAPONS OF WAR
SMALL ARMS
1950–PRESENT

✪ WEAPONS OF WAR
SMALL ARMS
1950–PRESENT

CHARTWELL
BOOKS

This edition published in 2013 by

CHARTWELL BOOKS
an imprint of Book Sales
a division of Quarto Publishing Group USA Inc.
142 West 36th Street, 4th Floor
New York, New York 10018
USA

Contributing authors: Chris Chant, Steve Crawford, Martin J. Dougherty, Ian Hogg,
Robert Jackson, Chris McNab, Michael Sharpe, Philip Trewhitt

ISBN 978-0-7858-2998-0

Printed in China

PICTURE CREDITS
Photographs:
Art-Tech/Aerospace: 8, 12–17 all, 21
Cody Images: 10
Corbis: 23 (Kate Brooks)
U.S. Department of Defense: 6, 7, 9, 11, 18–20 all, 22

Illustrations: © Art-Tech/Aerospace

CONTENTS

INTRODUCTION   6

Handguns   24
Manually Operated Rifles   56
Semi-auto and Automatic Rifles   65
Submachine Guns   116
Machine Guns   135
Grenade Launchers   161
Shotguns   166

INDEX   174

Introduction

Modern Guns

Modern small arms are more potent than ever, putting massive firepower at the disposal of individual soldiers.

The term 'small arms' was coined long ago to describe firearms that could be carried by a single person, i.e., gunpowder weapons lighter than artillery. Over the years, distinct types of small arms began to appear, each optimized to a particular role. The line between artillery and small arms was blurred when firearms heavy enough to be classed as support weapons began to appear. Light enough to move with infantry, but more potent than standard personal weapons, battlefield support weapons greatly increased the firepower of an infantry force.

The invention of personal automatic weapons was another profound leap forward. Where previously, group action was necessary to provide intense firepower, now a single individual could target multiple

KALASHNIKOV AK: see pages 70–71

M16: see page 74

L1A1 SLR: see page 66

WEAPONS OF WAR

The increased frequency of urban combat has hugely influenced the development of modern small arms.

opponents or deliver suppressing fire into an area. The increasing frequency of urban combat during World War II was another influence on the development of small arms and infantry support weapons. Whereas previously most engagements were at relatively long ranges of several hundred metres, which required accurate aimed rifle fire, urban battles were characterized by vicious short-range firefights. During the battle for Stalingrad, for example, German troops armed with bolt-action

rifles found themselves outgunned in such engagements by Red Army soldiers armed with submachine guns. Swapping rifles for submachine guns would have been an effective counter for urban combat, but in longer-range engagements, the rifle was still the weapon of choice. The answer was an intermediate weapon: smaller, lighter and faster firing than the traditional battle rifle, but still retaining good accuracy out to a respectable range, with reasonable penetrating power. Thus was born the

H&K G3: see page 75

FAMAS: see page 91

WEAPONS OF WAR

assault rifle and with it came a change in emphasis from groups of riflemen trained to a high standard of marksmanship towards smaller units capable of delivering intense firepower within their local vicinity.

COMBAT EFFECTIVENESS

A group of militia or gunmen will normally fight as individuals with whatever weapons they can get, but formal military forces are organized in a way that optimizes the effectiveness of their weapons. Various approaches have been tried in order to obtain maximum combat effectiveness, and the success of one does not necessarily mean another is wrong.

Typically, an infantry squad consists mainly of riflemen armed with a basic personal weapon; usually an assault rifle. The squad will normally contain a support weapon of some kind. This may be a general-purpose machine gun (GPMG) or a lighter squad support weapon. GPMGs tend to be chambered for battle rifle calibres; their ammunition is not compatible with the lighter cartridges used in assault weapons. However, GPMGs are powerful and offer good sustained firepower, out to ranges that lighter weapons cannot effectively reach.

Squad (or light) support weapons are sometimes little more than a variant of the standard infantry rifle, which has the advantage that magazines can be shared and any soldier can take over the support weapon. Mobility is better, too, since the weapon is lighter. However, a light support weapon does not have the hitting power or the sustained firepower of a GPMG.

Other weapons are generally used for supporting purposes. Handguns are carried

BERETTA MODEL 92SB: see page 47

STERLING L2A1: see page 117

as sidearms, shotguns are primarily used for security (and sometimes counter-ambush) applications, and an infantry force may be supported by grenade launchers and/or personnel armed with extremely accurate and often high-powered precision rifles.

Other approaches have been used, and successfully. For example, Chinese forces in the Korean conflict made extensive use of massed submachine guns in the assault role, while the British Army long considered marksmanship with a semi-automatic rifle more effective than automatic suppressive fire.

ASSAULT RIFLE SUPREME

With the end of World War II, most major powers were starting to recognise that the assault rifle would become the best infantry weapon, situated as it was between the pistol-calibre, short-range submachine gun and the long-range rifle. In 1947, the most

BERETTA MODEL 12: see page 122

famous assault rifle of all time was produced by Mikhail Timofeyevich Kalashnikov – the AK-47. It fired a 7.62mm intermediate cartridge and impressed the world with its ability to deliver heavy individual firepower while enduring the worst battlefield conditions.

Although it would later catch up, the newly formed NATO missed a bold chance to match the AK-47's useful cartridge with something similar by agreeing to standardise all NATO weapons to 7.62 x 51mm NATO. This round was over-powerful for an assault rifle with automatic capabilities, but certain US parties were reluctant to give up the long-range round. Many fine weapons were produced for this calibre – the US M14, the superb FN FAL and Heckler & Koch's G3 – but they all struggled under fully automatic fire.

The solution had begun to emerge from the US shortly after the Korean War. Research had begun into small-calibre high-velocity (1000mps/3200fps) ammunition, specifically the 5.56mm round. A rifle to fire this round was found in Eugene Stoner's AR-15, which would become the M16 rifle after it was adopted by the US Air Force in the early 1960s. The M16 used a highly efficient gas-operation and could fire easily on full automatic. Furthermore, the velocity of the small round was such that it retained the stopping and killing power of much larger rounds by force of its supersonic shock effect.

The 5.56mm round was resisted for many years (its cause not helped by early jamming problems with the M16), yet, after the US Army adopted it for general use in the M16A1 in Vietnam, the direction was

UZI: see page 119

L7A1: see page 142

WEAPONS OF WAR

PKM 7.62MM: see page 144

inexorable. In the late 1970s, the Soviet Union brought out a 5.45mm version of the AK-47, the AK-74; after trials in the 1980s, the 5.56 x 45mm round was adopted as the NATO standard. New weapons emerged. Heckler & Koch brought out the G41, the FN FAL rifle became the FN FNC and Israel produced the Galil.

'Bullpup' designs also gained currency. These were weapons that located much of the receiver behind the trigger unit and thus were able to maximise the length of the barrel for accuracy, while restraining the overall length of the weapon. Some of these designs – particularly the British Enfield L85A1, the French FAMAS and the Austrian Steyr AUG – have become standard-issue infantry weapons in some armies.

OTHER WEAPONS

While assault rifles have generally eclipsed submachine guns in their prominence following World War II, submachine gun technology and designs also proceeded apace. Perhaps the greatest development is in the area of compaction. High-quality submachine guns such as the Heckler & Koch MP5 series retain more rifle-like proportions, but other submachine guns have become little bigger than pistols. By siting the magazine within the pistol grip and using a telescoping bolt (i.e. a bolt which actually encloses the end of the barrel), guns such as the Uzi, the Ingram M10 and the South African BXP are easily concealed, yet can spray out devastating firepower in close-combat situations.

At the other end of the scale, standard assault rifles have also been developed with longer, heavier barrels to become squad

M60: see page 138

WEAPONS OF WAR

MINIGUN: see page 147

Some standard assault rifles have been developed as squad automatic weapons to provide supporting fire for infantry units.

automatic weapons (SAWs). These are intended to give small infantry units greater sustained-fire capability and range with their standard calibre weapons and from standard magazines. The jury is still out as to whether they perform a valuable function over the general purpose machine gun (GPMG) type that has been used as a heavier support weapon by most armies since World War II.

The astonishing scientific progress in terms of ballistics, materials and manufacturing in the twentieth and

twenty-first centuries means that even the humble pistol is a work of mastery. Modern handguns such as the SIG-Sauer P226 have 15-round magazines or, like the Glock pistol range, a higher percentage of their build in plastic than in metal. Sniper rifles have gone even further. The contemporary sniper armed with, say, an FR-F1 or an L96A1 and looking through an advanced-optics telescopic sight can confidently expect a first-round kill at 800m (2624ft), while, in the Gulf War, a sniper armed with a

REMINGTON M870: see page 166

Barrett .50in rifle took a confirmed kill at 1800m (5905ft).

THE FUTURE

The big question is, what next? In terms of weapons that use conventional ammunition and methods of operation, we have perhaps gone as far as we can. Recent experiments have been conducted using machine guns that fire bullets through electromagnetic acceleration rather than percussion, the result being an utterly silent, yet astonishingly dense and powerful rain of high-velocity fire. Other ideas are already off the drawing board. Heckler & Koch's G11 rifle fires caseless ammunition in which the bullet is embedded in a rectangle of propellant that disappears completely on firing. The removal of the need for ejection gives the rifle a very high rate of fire – its three-round burst sounds as a single explosion. Electro-magnetic propulsion weapons, however, might one day do away with propellants altogether. As history has shown, progress in weapons design is inexorable, and the next stage will soon be with us. In the final analysis, although the capabilities of a weapon are important, what really matters is the user. Good tactics and skilled marksmanship can overcome the limitations of a mediocre weapon system. It is when training, tactics and fighting spirit are combined with an effective weapon that great things are achieved.

BARRETT M82A1: see page 96

Tokagypt 58

The ubiquity of the 9mm Parabellum cartridge in modern pistols formed the basis of this Egyptian weapon, which is essentially a copy of the Soviet Tokarev TT-33 pistol for the 9mm round. 'Copy' is an accurate term, for, apart from the butt grip and finish, there is little to distinguish it from the Soviet original in either action or performance (hence the hybrid name, 'Toka-gypt'). Yet the change to a much more practical calibre has made a difference to its performance, and the gun was a decent weapon that ultimately had an inauspicious record of use. It was actually built in Hungary during the 1960s, but its intended user, the Egyptian Army, finally decided against the weapon as an issue firearm. The surplus stock was thus disseminated throughout the Egyptian police and also to various commercial parties in Western Europe.

SPECIFICATIONS

COUNTRY OF ORIGIN: Egypt/Hungary
CALIBRE: 9mm Parabellum
LENGTH: 194mm (7.65in)
WEIGHT: 0.91kg (2.01lb)
BARREL: 114mm (4.48in), 6 grooves, rh
FEED: 7-round detachable box magazine
OPERATION: short recoil
MUZZLE VELOCITY: 350mps (1150fps)
EFFECTIVE RANGE: 30m (98ft)
CYCLIC RATE OF FIRE: not applicable

Stechkin

The Stechkin was one of the Soviet Union's less successful postwar experiments in small arms design. The intention was to create a compact machine pistol with a fairly high rate of fire; this was pursued by producing a gun roundly based on the Walther PP, but with full-auto capability. It worked by blowback, using the mid-powered 9mm Soviet cartridge and could be fitted with a shoulder stock to give the user greater control during automatic fire, which had a cyclical rate of 850rpm. The Stechkin, however, was effectively too small for a machine pistol and too big for a pistol. It was fairly uncontrollable on full automatic and too bulky for conventional handling as a self-loading weapon, thereby satisfying nobody. Nonetheless, it stayed in production between 1951 and 1975, before finally being withdrawn from troop use.

SPECIFICATIONS

COUNTRY OF ORIGIN: Soviet Union/Russia
CALIBRE: 9mm Makarov
LENGTH: 225mm (8.86in)
WEIGHT: 1.03kg (2.27lb)
BARREL: 127mm (5in), 4 grooves, rh
FEED: 20-round detachable box magazine
OPERATION: blowback
MUZZLE VELOCITY: 340mps (1115fps)
EFFECTIVE RANGE: 30m (98ft)
CYCLIC RATE OF FIRE: 850rpm

Colt Python

Since its beginnings in 1955, the Colt Python has become one of the world's finest combat handguns. This reputation comes in the main from its high levels of workmanship and finish, and today it is made in either stainless steel or blued carbon steel. The gun's one drawback (apart from its very high price tag due to its quality of manufacture) is its high weight – around 1.16kg (2.56lb) – although this is an essential part of the gun's ability to fire the potent .357 Magnum round for which it is principally chambered. (A small batch of Pythons were made around the .38 Smith &Wesson cartridge.) This weight does, however, make the gun incredibly durable and, if the user is strong enough to handle it, then there are few guns that will give better, more consistent performance, and the Magnum round gives the Python a great deal of stopping power.

SPECIFICATIONS

COUNTRY OF ORIGIN: United States
CALIBRE: .357 Magnum
LENGTH: 235mm (9.25in) to 343mm (13.50in)
WEIGHT: 1.08kg (2.37lb) to 1.2kg (2.62lb)
BARREL: 102mm (4.02in); 204mm (8.03in)
FEED: 6 rounds
OPERATION: revolver
MUZZLE VELOCITY: 455mps (1500fps)
EFFECTIVE RANGE: 50m (164ft)
CYCLIC RATE OF FIRE: not applicable

Smith & Wesson Model 29 .44 Magnum

The power of the .44 Magnum handgun gained particular notoriety in the hands of Clint Eastwood in the 1970s, through his role in the popular 'Dirty Harry' movies (although Smith & Wesson actually launched the Model 29 back in 1955). The Model 29 came with a choice of three barrel lengths, ranging from the shortest – a 102mm (4.29in) version – to a striking 203mm (7.99in) version (which appeared in the films, and to which the specifications shown refer). Production of the Model 29 by Smith & Wesson has continued to this day in several different versions, now mostly designated as the 629 series. Most of the Model 29/629 series are distinguished by finish (the 629 first came out in stainless steel in 1979), barrel length or the positioning of the ejector rod, which is either shrouded or set into a recess underneath the barrel.

SPECIFICATIONS

COUNTRY OF ORIGIN: United States
CALIBRE: .44 Magnum
LENGTH: 353mm (13.89in)
WEIGHT: 1.45kg (3.19lb)
BARREL: 203mm (7.99in), 6 grooves, rh; also 153mm (6.02in) or 102mm (4.29in)
FEED: 6 rounds
OPERATION: revolver
MUZZLE VELOCITY: 450mps (1476fps)
EFFECTIVE RANGE: 50m (164ft)
CYCLIC RATE OF FIRE: not applicable

Astra Falcon

The Astra 'water pistol' design carried the company well through the first half of the 20th century. The Astra Falcon was the last pistol in that line. It appeared in the 1950s when Spain was still under Franco's rule, and is still in service today, owing to its solid build and its sound concept as an automatic handgun. In operation it is indistinguishable from the Astra 400; indeed, the Falcon is essentially the 400 design reduced considerably in length and weight to make it a handgun more suited to post-war police use. Whereas the 400 model was some 235mm (9.25in) long, the Falcon was scaled down to 164mm (6.4in) and its weight was reduced to a more comfortable 0.64kg (1.41lb). Unfortunately, the Astra Falcon is a lightweight gun in more than one respect, as its 9mm Short (.380 Auto) cartridge is generally a poor performer, and not well suited to the police role.

SPECIFICATIONS

COUNTRY OF ORIGIN: Spain
CALIBRE: 9mm Short (.380 Auto)
LENGTH: 164mm (6.46in)
WEIGHT: 0.64kg (1.41lb)
BARREL: 98.5mm (3.87in), 4 grooves, rh
FEED: 7-round detachable box magazine
OPERATION: blowback
MUZZLE VELOCITY: c.300mps (984fps)
EFFECTIVE RANGE: 30m (98ft)
CYCLIC RATE OF FIRE: not applicable

MBA Gyrojet 13mm

It is a contentious notion as to whether the Gyrojet is in fact a pistol at all. It is, in effect, a hand-held rocket launcher, the brainchild of two US inventors in the 1960s: Robert Mainhardt and Art Biehl. Instead of firing standard unitary cartridge rounds, the Gyrojet was designed to take 13 x 38mm projectiles, which consisted of a solid or explosive-filled head fixed into a tubular body that contained a propellant and had a baseplate containing a percussion cap and four thruster jet apertures. When fired, the percussion cap ignited the propellant, which in turn blasted the round out of the barrel. There being no cartridge to extract, the next round simply popped into the chamber ready for firing. Despite the fact that the jets were angled to give gyroscopic spin to the round in flight, the Gyrojet was not accurate and it never went beyond conceptual production.

SPECIFICATIONS

COUNTRY OF ORIGIN: United States
CALIBRE: 13mm rocket projectiles
LENGTH: 234mm (9.21in)
WEIGHT: 0.98kg (2.16lb)
BARREL: 127mm (5in)
FEED: 6-round detachable box magazine
OPERATION: short recoil
MUZZLE VELOCITY: 274mps (900fps)
EFFECTIVE RANGE: 50m (164ft)
CYCLIC RATE OF FIRE: not applicable

Smith & Wesson Mk 22

The infamous 'Hush Puppy' was born out of the demand by US Navy SEAL teams in Vietnam for an effective silenced pistol with which to dispose of Vietcong soldiers and sentry animals during covert missions. One answer was a suppressed Walther P38; the other was to extend the barrel of Smith & Wesson's Model 39 by 12.7cm (5in), thread the end and fit a silencer. With a slide lock and adjustable sights, and firing the subsonic Mark 144 Model 0 ammunition, this latter weapon became designated as the Mk22 Model 0 and was introduced into service in 1967. Known mainly by its nickname, the 'Hush Puppy' served the elite units well. Its muzzle velocity of 274mps (900fps) gave it enough power and range to be used at reasonable distances (accuracy allowing) and it stayed in military use until the 1980s.

SPECIFICATIONS

COUNTRY OF ORIGIN: United States
CALIBRE: 9mm Parabellum
LENGTH: 323mm (12.75in)
WEIGHT: 0.96kg (2.12lb)
BARREL: 101mm (3.98in) 6 grooves, rh
FEED: 8-round detachable box magazine
OPERATION: blowback
MUZZLE VELOCITY: 274mps (900fps)
EFFECTIVE RANGE: 30m (98ft)
CYCLIC RATE OF FIRE: semi-automatic

Heckler & Koch P9

The Heckler & Koch P9 comes in two versions: the standard P9 which is a single-action pistol (operation of the internal hammer is achieved by a release and cocking lever on the left side of the frame) and the P9S, which is a double-action weapon. What both have in common, however, is that they use the Heckler & Koch roller-locked delayed blowback system used in the G3 assault rifle. Thus, as recoil drives the bolt system rearwards, two rollers lock into barrel extensions and hold the bolt until pressure is at a safe level. Both the P9 and PS9 amount to fine handguns, used by several police and military units around the world; .45in calibre (for the US market) and 7.65mm Parabellum versions have also been issued. One item of note is that the bore has a polygonal configuration, with the rifling grooves set into the bore diameter.

SPECIFICATIONS

COUNTRY OF ORIGIN: Germany
CALIBRE: 9mm Parabellum or .45 ACP
LENGTH: 192mm (7.56in)
WEIGHT: 0.88kg (1.94lb)
BARREL: 102mm (4.02in), polygonal, rh
FEED: 9-round detachable box (9mm); 7-rnd detach. box (.45 ACP)
OPERATION: roller-locked delayed blowback
MUZZLE VELOCITY: 350mps (1150fps)
EFFECTIVE RANGE: 40m (131ft)
CYCLIC RATE OF FIRE: not applicable

Smith & Wesson 459

The Model 459 was one of Smith & Wesson's contributions to the US Army pistol trials in the 1980s, an event that turned into an acrimonious legal action after the company were quickly rejected in favour of European weapons manufacturers (Beretta were the final winners with their 92SB model). Smith & Wesson's original entry was the 469, but after this fell by the wayside in the first contest, the 459 was substituted and submitted into the second. The 459's heritage lies in the Model 39, produced between 1954 and 1980. This was a 9mm gun, used by the US Navy and Special Forces, but which became limited through only having an 8-round magazine. To rectify this, a 14-round version was produced – the Model 59 – and an improved version of this became the 459. Both the Model 59 and 459 were designed specifically for military use.

SPECIFICATIONS

COUNTRY OF ORIGIN: United States
CALIBRE: 9mm Parabellum
LENGTH: 175mm (6.89in)
WEIGHT: 0.73kg (1.61lb)
BARREL: 89mm (3.50in), 6 grooves, rh
FEED: 14-round detachable box magazine
OPERATION: blowback
MUZZLE VELOCITY: 395mps (1295fps)
EFFECTIVE RANGE: 40m (131ft)
CYCLIC RATE OF FIRE: not applicable

Helwan

The Helwan was a direct copy of Beretta's excellent Model M951 pistol for the Egyptian armed forces during the latter's build up; it was made under licence during the 1960s, chosen for service ahead of the Tokagypt. Being a direct copy, to describe its properties is to describe those of the original Beretta pistol, and the only way to distinguish the Helwan from the Beretta is by the inscription 'HELWAN CAL 9 m/m U.A.R.' on the weapon's slide. The Beretta M951/Helwan is a short-recoil pistol in which the locking of barrel and breech is achieved by locking lugs dropping into slots in the walls of the slide. Although Beretta originally – unsuccessfully – attempted to produce the M951 in a light alloy, the final steel gun was a solid first foray into a 9mm weapon for Beretta, and Israel also adopted the design for service.

SPECIFICATIONS

COUNTRY OF ORIGIN: Egypt
CALIBRE: 9 x 19mm Parabellum
LENGTH: 203mm (7.99in)
WEIGHT: 0.89kg (1.96lb)
BARREL: 114mm (4.48in), 6 grooves, rh
FEED: 8-round detachable box magazine
OPERATION: short recoil
MUZZLE VELOCITY: 350mps (1148fps)
EFFECTIVE RANGE: 40m (131ft)
CYCLIC RATE OF FIRE: not applicable

Ruger Security Six

The Ruger Security Six is a very powerful weapon, a power which it derives from its potent .357 Magnum round with its awesome stopping ability. The gun was produced by Ruger from 1968, but the design actually came from an earlier single-action revolver that was developed in the 1950s. Ruger's intention behind the Security Six was to create a quality handgun for use as a standard police weapon. The choice of round gave police officers a more versatile response than lighter calibres such as the .38, which had reduced penetrative power when fired against vehicles or other light constructions such as buildings. Sturm, Ruger & Co. has continued to make .357 weapons for the police market, and today models such as the GP100 are continuing to build Ruger's reputation for accuracy and controlled power in its handguns.

SPECIFICATIONS

COUNTRY OF ORIGIN: United States
CALIBRE: .357 Magnum
LENGTH: 235mm (9.25in)
WEIGHT: 0.95kg (2.09lb)
BARREL: 102mm (4.02in), 6 grooves, rh
FEED: 6-round cylinder
OPERATION: revolver
MUZZLE VELOCITY: c.400mps (1312fps)
EFFECTIVE RANGE: 40m (131ft) plus
CYCLIC RATE OF FIRE: not applicable

Manurhin MR73

A French-designed revolver of excellent overall quality, the Manurhin MR73 is a versatile pistol, which is available in a variety of calibres and barrel lengths to suit different shooting requirements, both private and military. The engineering of elements such as the trigger system – which is very smooth, owing to a separate spring – and barrel, which is cold-hammered, is especially fine. In fact, the weapon possesses the facility for changing the .38 Special cylinder for a 9mm Parabellum cylinder in just a couple of minutes, giving the gun greater flexibility than the average revolver. Whether in these calibres or in the more common .357in Magnum, the Manurhin MR73 is an accurate and stable weapon to fire, even when fitted with the shorter barrels favoured by the police and military for ease of concealment and lighter weight.

SPECIFICATIONS

COUNTRY OF ORIGIN: France
CALIBRE: .357 Magnum; .38 Special; 9mm Parabellum
LENGTH: 195mm (7.67in)
WEIGHT: 0.88kg (1.94lb)
BARREL: 63.5mm (2.5in)
FEED: 6 rounds
OPERATION: revolver
MUZZLE VELOCITY: according to cartridge
EFFECTIVE RANGE: according to cartridge
CYCLIC RATE OF FIRE: not applicable

PSM

The PSM (Pistolet Samozaryadniy Malogabaritniy, meaning 'Pistol, Self-Loading, Small') appears to have been designed with concealability in mind, as it has a narrow frame and smooth surfaces, and mainly (to our knowledge in the West) entered service with the Soviet police forces and special military units. It has since gone on to be a part of criminal kit throughout central Europe and modern-day Russia. The PSM is a double-action blowback weapon working on the rather low-powered 5.45mm Soviet Pistol cartridge. In overall appearance and much of its action, it resembles the Walther PP, but it does not appear to have the sophistication and quality inherent in the German weapon. Nevertheless, the PSM will probably have a long service life, if only in the hands of criminals, who can conveniently fit it into a pocket.

SPECIFICATIONS

COUNTRY OF ORIGIN: Soviet Union/Russia
CALIBRE: 5.45mm Soviet Pistol
LENGTH: 160mm (6.29in)
WEIGHT: 0.46kg (1.01lb)
BARREL: 85mm (3.35in), 6 grooves, rh
FEED: 8-round detachable box magazine
OPERATION: blowback
MUZZLE VELOCITY: 315mps (1033fps)
EFFECTIVE RANGE: 40m (131ft)
CYCLIC RATE OF FIRE: not applicable

CZ75

Since it first appeared in 1975, the CZ75 has excelled as both a combat and a commerical pistol, and has been much copied (made easier by the manufacturer's lack of effective patent cover outside Eastern Europe). It is based on the Colt-Browning dropping barrel action and has a double-action trigger mechanism. In terms of its action, there is little unusual to note, but the overall workmanship of the gun is high, and so the weapon gives the reliability and consistent performance required by military and police personnel. Ironically, the Czech military did not adopt the pistol (mainly because they followed Soviet calibrations), but many other world armies have taken the gun into service, either in its original format or as a copy (licensed or otherwise). A new model, the CZ85, has improved on the safety features.

SPECIFICATIONS

COUNTRY OF ORIGIN: Czechoslovakia
CALIBRE: 9mm Parabellum
LENGTH: 203mm (7.99in)
WEIGHT: 0.98kg (2.16lb)
BARREL: 120mm (4.72in), 6 grooves, rh
FEED: 15-round detachable box magazine
OPERATION: short recoil
MUZZLE VELOCITY: 338mps (1110fps)
EFFECTIVE RANGE: 40m (131ft)
CYCLIC RATE OF FIRE: not applicable

SIG-Sauer P-225

The SIG-Sauer P-225 shares the P-220's superlative reputation for quality, accuracy and reliability. It is actually a slightly compressed version of the P-220, losing nearly 2cm (0.78in) in length, and was developed to equip the West German police in the 1970s. That particular client needed a gun with failure-proof safety systems, so SIG-Sauer introduced a new automatic locking system for the firing pin, which meant that – even if the hammer were accidentally knocked forwards – the gun would not fire. The West German police service accepted the gun, as did the Swiss police, various US security agencies and, it is rumoured, certain US special forces units. Magazine capacity in the P-225 remained at eight 9mm rounds; subsequently, the P-226 variant took that capacity up to 15 rounds to make it more suitable for military use.

SPECIFICATIONS

COUNTRY OF ORIGIN: Switzerland (SIG); Germany (J. P. Sauer & Sohn)
CALIBRE: 9mm Parabellum
LENGTH: 180mm (7.08in)
WEIGHT: 0.74kg (1.63lb)
BARREL: 98mm (3.85in), 6 grooves, rh
FEED: 8-round detachable box magazine
OPERATION: short recoil
MUZZLE VELOCITY: 340mps (1115fps)
EFFECTIVE RANGE: 40m (131ft)
CYCLIC RATE OF FIRE: not applicable

MAB PA-15

MAB stands for Manufacture d'Armes de Bayonne, a long-standing French weapons producer who supplied the French forces with a standard service pistol, the PA-15, for more than two decades. The PA-15 was visually stylish and worked its way through a number of calibres, first starting with the 7.65mm ACP and 9mm Short cartridges, and then adopting the standard 9mm Parabellum round. In this latter calibration, the PA-15 had to work on a delayed blowback system of operation using a rotating barrel. The initial forces of recoil hold both slide and barrel locked in place through a grooved track until the bullet has left the muzzle, then pressures drop and the barrel turns, allowing the slide to recoil. The PA-15 gave good service in the French Army between 1975 and 1990, but its manufacturer, MAB, no longer exists.

SPECIFICATIONS

COUNTRY OF ORIGIN: France
CALIBRE: 9 x 19mm Parabellum
LENGTH: 203mm (7.99in)
WEIGHT: 1.07kg (2.36lb)
BARREL: 114mm (4.49in), 6 grooves, rh
FEED: 15-round detachable box magazine
OPERATION: delayed blowback
MUZZLE VELOCITY: 330mps (1100fps)
EFFECTIVE RANGE: 40m (131ft)
CYCLIC RATE OF FIRE: not applicable

Beretta Model 81

The Beretta Model 81 was developed and brought into service in the mid 1970s, part of Beretta's move towards double-action handguns with a greater rate of fire. Two models were brought out at this time: the Model 81 in 7.65mm calibre and the Model 84 for 9mm Short ammunition. Despite its age, the Model 81 is a thoroughly modern pistol in its design. It has a 12-round magazine capacity, and its double-fire action allows the user to pull the trigger twice on the same round in the case of a first-attempt misfire. Safety for users is also improved. The pistol cannot be fired if the magazine has been removed from the gun, even if a round is still seated in the chamber. The extractor protrudes from the weapon and shows red if there is a round in the chamber and the safety switch can be easily reached by both left- and right-handed shooters.

SPECIFICATIONS

COUNTRY OF ORIGIN: Italy
CALIBRE: 7.65mm
LENGTH: 172mm (6.77in)
WEIGHT: 0.65kg (1.43lb)
BARREL: 97mm (3.81in), 6 grooves, rh
FEED: 12-round detachable box magazine
OPERATION: blowback
MUZZLE VELOCITY: 300mps (985fps)
EFFECTIVE RANGE: 30m (98ft)
CYCLIC RATE OF FIRE: not applicable

Heckler & Koch P7

The P7 was purpose-designed for the Federal German Police by Heckler & Koch as a very safe, but rapid-response combat weapon. Two features distinguish this gun from other security handguns: the cocking lever and the mode of operation. The cocking lever is situated just in front of the grip. When out, it entirely prohibits the firing of the gun even if there is a round in the chamber. To fire, the user must squeeze in the grip to cock the firing pin before pulling the trigger. This gives a weapon that is very safe when not in use, but which can quickly be brought into action when need be. The operation is gas-actuated delayed blowback, in which gases are channelled from the barrel to momentarily resist the slide's recoil until the round has left the muzzle. This excellent, well-designed and popular weapon has entered broad global use.

SPECIFICATIONS

COUNTRY OF ORIGIN: Germany
CALIBRE: 9mm Parabellum
LENGTH: 171mm (6.73in)
WEIGHT: 0.8kg (1.76lb)
BARREL: 105mm (4.13in), polygonal, rh
FEED: 13-round detachable box magazine
OPERATION: gas-actuated delayed blowback
MUZZLE VELOCITY: 350mps (1150fps)
EFFECTIVE RANGE: 40m (131ft)
CYCLIC RATE OF FIRE: not applicable

SMALL ARMS 1950–PRESENT HANDGUNS

Walther P5

The Walther P5 was produced by the company in the 1970s to meet the demanding safety criteria of the West German police, who were looking for a new handgun. The gun's actual firing mechanism is essentially that of the excellent Walther P38, but with three specific safety features. First, only if the trigger is pulled, will the firing pin strike the cartridge, as usually the firing pin sits in a recess in the hammer; pulling the trigger realigns the firing pin with the impact portion of the hammer. Added to this is a safety notch for the hammer, and the gun will not fire unless the slide is in a fully closed position. In addition to its first-class safety precautions, the P5 is also a splendid weapon to fire, and its overall fine qualities have taken it into service outside Germany, in countries such as Portugal and Holland.

SPECIFICATIONS

COUNTRY OF ORIGIN: Germany
CALIBRE: 9mm Parabellum
LENGTH: 180mm (7.08in)
WEIGHT: 0.79kg (1.75lb)
BARREL: 90mm (3.54in), 6 grooves, rh
FEED: 8-round detachable box magazine
OPERATION: short recoil
MUZZLE VELOCITY: 350mps (1150fps)
EFFECTIVE RANGE: 40m (131ft)
CYCLIC RATE OF FIRE: not applicable

Heckler & Koch P11

The P11 is one of the most distinctive weapons from the Heckler & Koch stable. It is an underwater pistol, designed specifically for use by special forces operatives. Developed during the 1970s, it is a multi-barrel weapon, each of the five barrels protected by a thin waterproof diaphragm and holding a 7.62mm (0.3in) drag-stabilized dart. The powder charges in the darts are ignited electronically by the pistol's two AA batteries, and the effective range of the pistol under water is about 15m (49ft), double that distance above water. Note that the barrel block, once empty, is not reloaded by the user, but is replaced by another barrel block. Details about the P11 are not complete, but it has entered service with naval Special Forces in the US, UK, Italy, France, Norway and Germany, and rivals the Russian SSP-1M in the underwater pistol market.

SPECIFICATIONS

COUNTRY OF ORIGIN: Germany
CALIBRE: 7.62mm (0.3in)
LENGTH: 200mm (7.87in)
WEIGHT: c. 1.2kg (2.65lb)
BARREL: n/a
FEED: 5-round detachable barrel block
OPERATION: electric ignition
MUZZLE VELOCITY: not available
EFFECTIVE RANGE: c. 15m (49ft) underwater
CYCLIC RATE OF FIRE: not applicable

Ruger Redhawk

Sturm, Ruger & Company's first double-action revolvers were the Security Six, Police Six and Speed Six, which emerged in the 1970s, but are now discontinued; the Redhawk was a continuation of the theme of a powerful .44 Magnum handgun for use primarily by hunters in the US rather than the military. The potential force within the gun is indicated by the Redhawk model's integral telescopic sight mounts being cut into the length of the barrel. The sight coupled with the powerful round enable the Ruger to be turned into a hunting weapon with an effective range of around 60m (197ft). To take the .44 round's power, the barrel has an increased wall thickness just in front of the chamber. The Redhawk's combination of compactness and sheer brute power has made it a popular weapon for commercial users throughout the world.

SPECIFICATIONS

COUNTRY OF ORIGIN: United States
CALIBRE: .44 Magnum
LENGTH: 165mm (6.49in)
WEIGHT: 1.5kg (3.37lb)
BARREL: 190mm (7.48in)
FEED: 6 rounds
OPERATION: revolver
MUZZLE VELOCITY: 450mps (1475fps)
EFFECTIVE RANGE: 60m (197ft)
CYCLIC RATE OF FIRE: not applicable

IMI Desert Eagle

P art of a modern return to vogue of large-calibre combat pistols, the Desert Eagle originated in the US, but went through to production at Israel Military Industries (IMI) in Israel. It comes in three main Magnum calibres – .357, .44 and .50 – all of which produce a conclusive stopping power. The mechanism of the Desert Eagle is gas-operated. On firing, gas is drawn off through a port just in front of the chamber; this pushes back the slide, which ejects the spent round from the chamber, then returns and reloads the weapon under the pressure of a return spring. The gas bleed reduces the significant recoil of the Desert Eagle to manageable levels for the firer, but it is still an incredibly powerful weapon – it can even come with extended barrels and telescopic sights – which has yet to persuade military circles of its validity.

SPECIFICATIONS

COUNTRY OF ORIGIN: United States/Israel
CALIBRE: .357in, .44in or .50in Magnum
LENGTH: 260mm (10.25in)
WEIGHT: 1.7kg (3.75lb) .357; 1.8kg (3.97lb) .44; 2.05kg (4.52lb) .50
BARREL: 152mm (5.98in)
FEED: 9 rounds (.357 Mag); 8 rounds (.44 Mag); 7 rounds (.50 Mag)
OPERATION: gas
MUZZLE VELOCITY: 436mps (1430fps) for .357 Magnum; 448mps (1470fps) .44 Magnum
EFFECTIVE RANGE: 50m (164ft) plus
CYCLIC RATE OF FIRE: not applicable

Glock 17

A remarkable weapon in terms of construction, materials and marketing, the Glock 17 has become a dominant force in the military and commercial handgun industries since its introduction. First produced in 1983, it demonstrates a 40 per cent use of plastic materials (although the barrel and slide naturally remain metal) and an inventory of only 33 parts for each gun. While the plastic makes it a light weapon, the Glock 17 also has an impressive magaxine capacity of no less than 17 rounds and fires its ammunition using a trigger-controlled striker instead of a hammer. It uses a locked breech with tilting barrel mechanism and safety is provided by a trigger safety and firing-pin lock. Through good marketing, and following its adoption by the Austrian Army, the Glock 17 has gone on to extensive military and police use across the world.

SPECIFICATIONS

COUNTRY OF ORIGIN: Austria
CALIBRE: 9mm Parabellum
LENGTH: 188mm (7.40in)
WEIGHT: 0.65kg (1.44lb)
BARREL: 114mm (4.49in), 6 grooves, rh
FEED: 17-round detachable box magazine
OPERATION: short recoil
MUZZLE VELOCITY: 350mps (1148fps)
EFFECTIVE RANGE: 40m (131ft)
CYCLIC RATE OF FIRE: n/a

Beretta Model 92SB

The Beretta Model 92SB had the honour of winning the US Army's trials in the 1980s for a replacement side arm to the M1911, although some further modifications had to be made before it went into US service as the Model 92F. The 92SB is actually part of an extensive Model 92 series, all of superb quality and designed around a practical range of military and security needs. Origins of the 92 series began in an update of the Model 951 with a greater magazine capacity and a double action. Subsequent models improved on various elements and, by the time the 92SB reached the US trials, it had an ambidextrous safety and magazine catch and a half-cock facility. The 92F saw further modifications to satisfy US purchase demands, mainly limited to the gun's ergonomics, but also including the internal chroming of the barrel.

SPECIFICATIONS
COUNTRY OF ORIGIN: Italy
CALIBRE: 9mm Parabellum
LENGTH: 197mm (7.76in)
WEIGHT: 0.98kg (2.16lb)
BARREL: 109mm (4.29in), 6 grooves, rh
FEED: 13-round detachable box magazine
OPERATION: short recoil
MUZZLE VELOCITY: 385mps (1263fps)
EFFECTIVE RANGE: 40m (131ft)
CYCLIC RATE OF FIRE: not applicable

Beretta Model 93R

The Beretta 93R is an attempt to give a standard pistol greater capability in close-quarters combat by giving it a selective-fire facility. A switch on the side of the gun allows the user to choose between single shots and a three-round burst, the latter giving the weapon a cyclic rate of 1100rpm. Naturally, stability in the standard pistol configuration is compromised in such a mode, so the 93R features a folding foregrip just in front of the trigger that gives the automatic mode a genuine useability. The firer is able to control the weapon's recoil, meaning that the shots can be fired in a close grouping. Further control is added by the option of a folding metal stock and a short muzzle brake/flash hider. The 93R is used by some special forces in both Italy and abroad, but the concept of the pistol/ machine pistol has yet to gain worldwide currency.

SPECIFICATIONS

COUNTRY OF ORIGIN: Italy
CALIBRE: 9mm Parabellum
LENGTH: 240mm (9.45in)
WEIGHT: 1.12kg (2.47lb)
BARREL: 156mm (6.14in), 6 grooves, rh
FEED: 15- or 20-round detachable box
OPERATION: short recoil
MUZZLE VELOCITY: 375mps (1230fps)
EFFECTIVE RANGE: 40m (131ft)
CYCLIC RATE OF FIRE: 1100rpm

Glock 18

While, in 1986, Beretta were bringing out their fully automatic pistol, the Beretta 93R, Glock were also introducing their Model 18 handgun. This featured two extended magazine options – one with a 19-round capacity, the other holding as many as 33 rounds – and looked and worked very much like the Model 17 pistol. Yet, because of some internal modifications, the Glock 18 could fire at a high cyclic rate of around 1300rpm. Naturally, this fully automatic capability has taken the Glock 18 out of the commercial market in favour of government and military use. Whether these markets will find the gun practical only time will tell, but the rationale behind the fully automatic pistol, as opposed to simply having a small submachine gun, is questionable, as the former is difficult to control even if fired by an experienced shooter.

SPECIFICATIONS

COUNTRY OF ORIGIN: Austria
CALIBRE: 9mm Parabellum
LENGTH: 223mm (8.78in)
WEIGHT: 0.636kg (1.40lb)
BARREL: 114mm (4.49in), hexagonal, rh
FEED: 19- or 33-round detachable box magazine
OPERATION: short recoil
MUZZLE VELOCITY: 350mps (1148fps)
EFFECTIVE RANGE: 40m (131ft)
CYCLIC RATE OF FIRE: 1300rpm

Glock 20

From the early 1990s, a new range of Glock pistols appeared on the market in larger calibres than the traditional 9mm Parabellum. The Glock 20 and 21 were available in 10mm Auto, an especially powerful pistol round to be handled only by the well-trained shooter used to handling such weapons (it soon became an FBI handgun). Glock was amongst the first gun manufacturers to make a 10mm gun, but the Glock 20 retained all the features of earlier weapons: a two-part trigger for effective safety control, a large capacity (15-round) magazine, and an overall light weight (0.78kg/1.73lb) owing to its predominantly plastic construction. The Glock 20 was followed by another 10mm gun, the Glock 21, after which no's. 22 and 23 arrived in .40 Smith & Wesson calibre. A new version of the weapon is now being produced in .45 ACP.

SPECIFICATIONS

COUNTRY OF ORIGIN: Austria
CALIBRE: 10mm Auto
LENGTH: 193mm (7.59in)
WEIGHT: 0.78kg (1.73lb)
BARREL: 117mm (4.61in), hexagonal, rh
FEED: 15-round detachable box magazine
OPERATION: short recoil
MUZZLE VELOCITY: 350mps (1148fps)
EFFECTIVE RANGE: 40m (131ft)
CYCLIC RATE OF FIRE: not applicable

Calico M950

One of the most striking modern pistols, the Calico M950 strays towards the submachine gun category, even though it will only fire in a semi-automatic mode. As is evident from the illustration, the grip for the weapon is two-handed and, with the magazine, the length of the M950 extends to 365mm (14.37in). Undoubtedly, it is the feed system of the Calico that is its most distinctive feature. The 50- or 100-round helical magazines are fitted to the top of the weapon running lengthwise down the receiver (50-round magazines are the more standard). Weighing about 1.8kg (3.97lb) when loaded and 1kg (2.20lb) when empty), the M950 fires standard 9mm Parabellum rounds to an effective range of about 60m (197ft) on account of its longer barrel. An interesting weapon, the Calico's military markets are yet to be decided.

SPECIFICATIONS

COUNTRY OF ORIGIN: United States
CALIBRE: 9mm Parabellum
LENGTH: 365mm (14.37in)
WEIGHT: 1kg (2.20lb)
BARREL: 152mm (5.98in), 6 grooves, rh
FEED: 50- or 100-round detachable helical magazine
OPERATION: delayed blowback
MUZZLE VELOCITY: 393mps (1290fps)
EFFECTIVE RANGE: 60m (197ft)
CYCLIC RATE OF FIRE: not applicable

SIG-Sauer P-226

The SIG-Sauer P-226 very nearly became the US Army's standard handgun following the acrimonious pistol trials in the mid-1980s. It was only just beaten in the competition by the Beretta Model 92 on the issue of price alone, and its superb quality has seen the design taken into use among many US police and security agencies such as the FBI (whose agents use the gun with subsonic loads more appropriate to their police work). It relies heavily on parts from the earlier SIG P-220 and P-225 designs, yet it differs in several respects relevant to its original military intention. The magazine is expanded to take a full fifteen 9mm rounds, seven rounds more than the P-225. Furthermore, the gun is designed for ambidextrous use, with a magazine release on both sides of the gun just behind the trigger.

SPECIFICATIONS

COUNTRY OF ORIGIN: Switzerland
CALIBRE: 9 x 19mm Parabellum
LENGTH: 196mm (7.72in)
WEIGHT: 0.75kg (1.65lb)
BARREL: 112mm (4.41in), 6 grooves, rh
FEED: 15-round detachable box magazine
OPERATION: short recoil
MUZZLE VELOCITY: 350mps (1148fps)
EFFECTIVE RANGE: 40m (131ft)
CYCLIC RATE OF FIRE: not applicable

Star 30M

The Star 30M is an exceptional pistol, which first entered production in 1990 and is still going strong today in various commercial and military hands. On first glance, the 30M actually looks like a standard Browning imitation gun, but further examination shows that the weapon's slide is actually running inside the gun's frame instead of outside. This configuration gives the gun great stability when it is being fired, and therefore increased accuracy. The resultant performance and the double-action trigger system enabled the 30M to take the recent contract for a Spanish Army service pistol and it is likely that this excellent design will open up many export markets for Astra in the future. In addition to the all-steel 30M, there is a light alloy version available on the market known as the 30PK, which has a lighter overall weight.

SPECIFICATIONS

COUNTRY OF ORIGIN: Spain
CALIBRE: 9mm Parabellum
LENGTH: 205mm (8.07in)
WEIGHT: 1.14kg (2.51lb)
BARREL: 119mm (4.69in), 6 grooves, rh
FEED: 15-round detachable box magazine
OPERATION: blowback
MUZZLE VELOCITY: 380mps (1250fps)
EFFECTIVE RANGE: 40m (131ft)
CYCLIC RATE OF FIRE: not applicable

Smith & Wesson 1006

During the 1980s, Smith & Wesson introduced a Third Generation series of pistols in various calibres ranging from 9mm to .45 ACP and including, in the case of the 1006, a 10mm Auto weapon. This was not the first 10mm development in the history of handguns – the US company Dornaus & Dixon produced one, the Bren 10, in the early 1980s – but this ceased production when the company went into receivership in 1985. By this time, however, the FBI were interested in the potential of the 10mm gun and so Smith & Wesson produced the 1006 from 1990. The calibre makes the gun very powerful indeed, but good-quality Novak sights and combat grips make it controllable in trained hands. The numbering system is part of Smith & Wesson's Third Generation notation, the first two digits indicating the calibre of the weapon.

SPECIFICATIONS

COUNTRY OF ORIGIN: United States
CALIBRE: 10mm Auto
LENGTH: 216mm (8.50in)
WEIGHT: 1.07kg (2.37lb)
BARREL: 127mm (5in), 6 grooves, rh
FEED: short recoil
OPERATION: 9-round detachable box magazine
MUZZLE VELOCITY: 335mps (1100fps)
EFFECTIVE RANGE: 30m (98ft)
CYCLIC RATE OF FIRE: not applicable

FN Five-Seven

While most modern semi-automatic handguns tend to use the 9mm or .45in cartridges, the FN Five-Seven actually uses the 5.7 x 28mm FN round, the same as that found in Fabrique Nationale's P90 personal defence weapon. Combined with a 20-round magazine, the result is an extremely potent handgun for military and police use. To handle the cartridge safely, the Five-Seven works on a delayed-blowback principle; the barrel and the slide hold together after firing until the gas pressure has reached safe levels, at which point the slide disengages and performs the full spent-case ejection and reloading cycle. Another notable feature of this handgun is the complete absence of safety switch. The Five-Seven is a self-cocking handgun – trigger pressure alone draws back and releases the firing pin, hence a safety switch is seen as unnecessary.

SPECIFICATIONS

COUNTRY OF ORIGIN: Belgium
CALIBRE: 5.7 x 28mm FN
LENGTH: 208mm (8.18in)
WEIGHT: 0.62kg (1.36lb)
BARREL: 122.5mm (4.82in)
FEED: 20-round detachable box magazine
OPERATION: delayed blowback
MUZZLE VELOCITY: 650mps (2133fps)
EFFECTIVE RANGE: 50m (164ft)
CYCLIC RATE OF FIRE: not applicable

M40A1

The M40 was a specific selection of the US Marine Corps in 1966 and is essentially a standard Remington Model 700 adapted for military use. The M40 was a superb weapon by all accounts and authorities, and met the high standards placed on it by the exhaustively trained Marine snipers. It featured a Mauser-type bolt action and a heavy barrel, with a five-round magazine. The M40A1 is an improved version of this gun. The heavy barrel has given way to a stainless steel barrel and the furniture is now made out of the lighter fibreglass, rather than wood, which improves its handling. In addition, whereas the M40 used a Redfield zoom telescopic sight that could reach x 9 magnification, the latest sight climbs to x 10 magnification. This sight obviates the need for the iron sight fitting that can be seen on some of the earliest M40 models.

SPECIFICATIONS

COUNTRY OF ORIGIN: United States
CALIBRE: 7.62 x 51mm NATO
LENGTH: 1117mm (43.98in)
WEIGHT: 6.57kg (14.48lb)
BARREL: 610mm (24.02in), 4 grooves, rh
FEED: 5-round integral box magazine
OPERATION: bolt action
MUZZLE VELOCITY: 777mps (2550fps)
EFFECTIVE RANGE: 800m (2624ft) plus
CYCLIC RATE OF FIRE: not applicable

Weatherby Mk V

The Weatherby Mk V is actually a sporting rifle used for hunting, not a military gun, but its capabilities are just as impressive and its overall quality of build and design is excellent. Its US designer was one Roy Weatherby and the Mk V designation is actually the name of the locking system used in the bolt action. This used some nine locking lugs configured to give the exceptionally smooth action that hunters appreciate when needing a rapid and solid reloading. As a commercial rifle, the Mk V has been through a bewildering variety of calibres to suit different pursuits and hunting limitations. These have ranged from .22–250 to the potent .460 Winchester Magnum calibre, and the consequent change of barrels means that there is much variety in the weight, velocity and effective range of Weatherby guns.

SPECIFICATIONS

COUNTRY OF ORIGIN: United States
CALIBRE: various
LENGTH: 1105mm (43.50in) to 1180mm (46.46in)
WEIGHT: 2.95kg (6.50lb) to 4.75kg (10.47lb)
BARREL: 610mm (24.02in) or 660mm (25.98in)
FEED: 5-round integral box magazine
OPERATION: bolt action
MUZZLE VELOCITY: various
EFFECTIVE RANGE: 1000m (3280ft) plus
CYCLIC RATE OF FIRE: not applicable

Steyr SSG 69

When the Steyr SSG 69 emerged as the Austrian Army's standard sniper rifle in 1969, it soon gathered a reputation as a well-crafted, robust and especially accurate bolt-action weapon. Equipped with the x 6 Kahles ZF69 sight, it could not only achieve a guaranteed first-round kill at 800m (2624ft), but it could also then place the next 10 rounds in a grouping of less than 400mm (15.75in) at the same range (the SSG 69 subsequently went on to be an internationally competitive target rifle). Being Austrian in origin, the SSG 69 had to be strong enough for use by mountain troops. The bolt action is of a rear-locking Mannlicher type using six locking lugs and it uses the pre–World War I Mannlicher rotary magazine (a standard 10-round box is also applicable), both unusual choices for a modern gun, but very strong in design. The SSG 69 is fully adjustable, including stock length.

SPECIFICATIONS

COUNTRY OF ORIGIN: Austria
CALIBRE: 7.62 x 51mm NATO
LENGTH: 1140mm (44.88in)
WEIGHT: 3.9kg (8.59lb)
BARREL: 650mm (25.59in), 4 grooves, rh
FEED: 5-round rotary or 10-round box magazine
OPERATION: bolt action
MUZZLE VELOCITY: 860mps (2820fps)
EFFECTIVE RANGE: 1000m (3280ft)
CYCLIC RATE OF FIRE: not applicable

FR-F1

The FR-F1 was a French sniper rifle developed in the 1960s and based on the MAS 36 service rifle. The redesign was extensive: the barrel was lengthened, the stock was given a cheek rest, the trigger unit acquired a pistol grip and the barrel a flash hider. All these improvements produced a sniper rifle of competition standard, yet there were some deficiencies. Principal among these was the retention of the ageing 7.5mm Mle 1929 French Service round while the rest of Europe was modelling its comparable weapons around the now-standard 7.62mm NATO calibre ammunition. Eventually, later models of the FR-F1 were made in the NATO calibre, and this was continued in the FR-F2 model, which replaced the FR-F1. Other problems with the FR-F1 included a rather excessive weight for its role and a somewhat insubstantial bipod.

SPECIFICATIONS

COUNTRY OF ORIGIN: France
CALIBRE: 7.5 x 54 Mle 1929 and 7.62 x 51mm NATO
LENGTH: 1138mm (44.80in)
WEIGHT: 5.2kg (11.46lb)
BARREL: 552mm (21.37in), 4 grooves, rh
FEED: 10-round integral box magazine
OPERATION: bolt action
MUZZLE VELOCITY: 852mps (2795fps)
EFFECTIVE RANGE: 800m (2624ft)
CYCLIC RATE OF FIRE: not applicable

Mauser SP66

The SP66 is one of Mauser's top-flight bolt-action sniper rifles, a heavily machined and prodigiously accurate weapon modified from a civilian hunting rifle. Sophistication runs through the weapon from muzzle to butt. The gun uses Mauser's short-action bolt operation, which allows the user to keep his head in place (and thus observing the target) while reloading. The stock is fully adjustable and has a thumb hold for extra grip control, and surfaces are deliberately roughened to aid overall hand adhesion. Sighting is done through a x 1.5–x 6 Zeiss-Divari telescopic sight (the gun can also accept almost any other sight commercially available) and the muzzle is fitted with a combined muzzle brake and flash reducer. The Mauser's only drawback is that the quality of the SP66 makes it an expensive weapon; Mauser make the 86SR as a less costly version.

SPECIFICATIONS

COUNTRY OF ORIGIN: Germany
CALIBRE: 7.62 x 51mm NATO
LENGTH: 1210mm (47.64in)
WEIGHT: 6.12kg (13.49lb) with telescopic sight
BARREL: 650mm (25.59in); 750mm (28.74in) with muzzle brake; 4 grooves, rh
FEED: 3-round integral box magazine
OPERATION: bolt action
MUZZLE VELOCITY: 868mps (2848fps)
EFFECTIVE RANGE: 1000m (3280ft)
CYCLIC RATE OF FIRE: not applicable

Parker-Hale Model 85

The Model 85 is one of a series of fine sniper and hunting weapons to emerge from the factories of Parker-Hale in recent years (although the manufacturer since 1990 is actually the Gibbs Rifle Co., USA). As a modern bolt-action sniper rifle, it is fairly standard; it has an adjustable butt and cheek rest, a detachable bipod and fires the 7.62mm NATO round. Yet the quality of its production, particularly in its heavy chrome-molybdenum free-floating barrel and Mauser-style bolt action, makes it very accurate indeed. The standard x6 telescopic sight can give a 100 per cent first-round hit rate at up to 600m (1969ft) and an 85 per cent hit rate at up to 900m (2953ft) when used by a skilled professional. Despite such sterling accuracy, the British Army, for whom the Model 85 was designed, rejected it in favour of the Accuracy International L96A1.

SPECIFICATIONS
COUNTRY OF ORIGIN: United Kingdom
CALIBRE: 7.62 x 51mm NATO
LENGTH: 1150mm (45.28in)
WEIGHT: 5.7kg (12.57lb) with telescopic sight
BARREL: 700mm (27.56in), 4 grooves, rh
FEED: 10-round box magazine
OPERATION: bolt action
MUZZLE VELOCITY: 860mps (2820fps)
EFFECTIVE RANGE: 1000m (3280ft) plus
CYCLIC RATE OF FIRE: not applicable

Accuracy International L96A1

The L96A1 entered production in 1985 as the replacement for the Lee-Enfield L42A1 as the British Army and Royal Marine's standard sniper rifle. It continues in 7.62mm NATO calibre, but, being descended from the Model PM – an Olympic-standard sports rifle – it has a new level of sophistication for a combat sniper weapon. The free-floating stainless steel barrel and Tasco sight give a 100 per cent hit rate at 600m (1968ft), while the stock is designed for ambidextrous use. The rifle is fitted with an alloy bipod and both rifle stripping and barrel change are simple tasks. Variants of the L96A1 include versions chambered for 7mm Remington Magnum, the .300 Winchester Magnum and .338 Lapua Magnum (rounds that give extra range), a single-shot long-range version and a silenced version, which uses subsonic ammunition.

SPECIFICATIONS

COUNTRY OF ORIGIN: United Kingdom
CALIBRE: 7.62mm NATO and others
LENGTH: 1163mm (45.78in)
WEIGHT: 6.2kg (13.68lb)
BARREL: 654mm (25.78in), 4 grooves, rh
FEED: 10-round detachable box magazine
OPERATION: bolt action
MUZZLE VELOCITY: 840mps (2830fps)
EFFECTIVE RANGE: 1000m (3280ft)
CYCLIC RATE OF FIRE: n/a

Beretta Sniper

Despite being a rather conventional rifle, the Beretta Sniper still possesses a very good performance, due in the main to Beretta's superb standards of workmanship and engineering. What it does have, however, is an advanced free-floating barrel design, in which a counterweight in the forestock serves almost to cancel out barrel vibrations upon firing for even greater accuracy. Generally used in a sniper role with the standard-issue Zeiss Divari Z telescopic sights, it can also be fitted with precision iron sights, which are capable of telling use in trained hands. The Beretta Sniper has not achieved great sales outside of Italian security use and appears to be a little undersold. Yet it is still a fine weapon compatible with standard NATO ammunition, so could make a more overt appearance in the world market in the future.

SPECIFICATIONS
COUNTRY OF ORIGIN: Italy
CALIBRE: 7.62 x 51mm NATO
LENGTH: 1165mm (45.87in)
WEIGHT: 5.55kg (12.23lb)
BARREL: 586mm (23.07in), 4 grooves, rh
FEED: 5-round detachable box magazine
OPERATION: bolt action
MUZZLE VELOCITY: 840mps (2755fps)
EFFECTIVE RANGE: 1000m (3280ft) plus
CYCLIC RATE OF FIRE: not applicable

Iver Johnson Model 500

The Model 500 is a .50in calibre sniper rifle, which developed out of the impressive Model 300. Why the Model 500 should have been developed when the Model 300 had serious knock-down power at 1500m (4921ft) is open to debate, but – whereas the Model 300 offered an acceptable performance – the Model 500 has been dogged by problems. The Model 500 is a truly advanced rifle, with a fluted and dampened heavy barrel and completely adjustable furniture. Such technologies, and the excellence of modern telescopic sights, have led the Model 500's manufacturers to claim an effective accuracy up to and over 2000m (6562ft). Yet it is unlikely that the Browning .50 machine-gun round could be controllable over such ranges and this, combined with the Model 500's enormous recoil and tendency to jam, has fettered the gun's commercial viability.

SPECIFICATIONS

COUNTRY OF ORIGIN: United States
CALIBRE: .50 BMG
LENGTH: 1200mm (47.24in)
WEIGHT: 13.6kg (29.98lb)
BARREL: 838mm (32.99in), rh
FEED: not known
OPERATION: bolt action
MUZZLE VELOCITY: 888mps (2914fps)
EFFECTIVE RANGE: 2000m (6562ft)
CYCLIC RATE OF FIRE: not applicable

FN FAL Para

The FN FAL rifle comes in a multitude of forms and formats, which vary depending on the country of use and the units for which it is destined. However, most standard FN FAL rifles are based around four key variants: the FN 50-00 (fixed stock, standard barrel); the FN 50-64 (side-folding stock, standard barrel); the FN 5041 (fixed stock, heavy barrel, bipod); and the FN 50-63 Para model. This last weapon was designed to provide a more compact rifle for special forces and airborne use, and featured a folding skeletal stock and a shortened barrel. These new dimensions did not bring the FN FAL's overall performance down, but they did reduce its stock extended length to 770mm (30.31in), which meant that the rifle was more portable. The Para rifle, like the other FN FAL models, has achieved extensive world-wide distribution during its lifetime.

SPECIFICATIONS

COUNTRY OF ORIGIN: Belgium
CALIBRE: 7.62 x 51mm NATO
LENGTH: 1020mm (40.16in) stock extended; 770mm (30.31in) stock folded
WEIGHT: 4.36kg (9.61lb)
BARREL: 436mm (17.17in) 4 grooves, rh
FEED: 20-round detachable box magazine
OPERATION: gas
MUZZLE VELOCITY: 853mps (2800)
EFFECTIVE RANGE: 900m (2953ft) plus
CYCLIC RATE OF FIRE: 650–700rpm

L1A1 Self-loading Rifle

The persuasive qualities of the Belgian FN FAL rifle led the British Army to adopt it as their standard service rifle from 1954, but licence-produced as the L1A1 Self-loading Rifle. The L1A1 had its dimensions slightly altered to suit manufacture in imperial measurements and would only fire semi-automatic. The L1A1 served British soldiers well across the world. On the streets of Northern Ireland, it was over-powerful, as it could easily command ranges of more than 800m (2624ft). Yet it left its mark in the Falklands War, when it could easily handle the distances between Argentine and British positions. The L1A1 was, however, a fearsome weapon to handle and needed substantial training. Although replaced by the 5.56mm L85A1 in the 1980s, it was used by special forces units in the Gulf War for its long range.

SPECIFICATIONS

COUNTRY OF ORIGIN: United Kingdom
CALIBRE: 7.62 x 51mm NATO
LENGTH: 1055mm (41.54in)
WEIGHT: 4.31kg (9.50lb)
BARREL: 535mm (21.06in), 4 grooves, rh
FEED: 20-round box magazine
OPERATION: gas
MUZZLE VELOCITY: 853mps (2800fps)
EFFECTIVE RANGE: 800m (2624ft) plus
CYCLIC RATE OF FIRE: semi-automatic only

CETME

The CETME takes its rank alongside the Heckler & Koch G3 and the FN FAL as one of the most widely used assault rifles, even though it perhaps did not quite achieve the level of popularity as these competitors. The CETME rifles actually originate from Mauser, which developed a prototype rifle during World War II. This prototype turned into a production model when the designers moved to fascist Spain's CETME concern following the end of the war. The CETME Model 58 series was the original. It first fired a 7.92mm round, then a special reduced-power 7.62mm round. Its operation was to be influential; the roller-locked delayed blowback came to be used by Heckler & Koch in some of their weapons. The subsequent history of the CETME rifles is one of recalibration. After changing to the full-power NATO round in 1974, the latest models (L and LC) use the standard 5.56mm NATO round.

SPECIFICATIONS

COUNTRY OF ORIGIN: Spain
CALIBRE: 7.92 x 51mm; 7.62 x 51mm NATO; 5.56 x 45mm NATO
LENGTH: 1015mm (39.96in)
WEIGHT: 4.5kg (9.92lb)
BARREL: 450mm (17.72in), 4 grooves, rh
FEED: 20-round detachable box magazine
OPERATION: gas, self-loading
MUZZLE VELOCITY: 7.92mm: 780mps (2560fps); 5.56mm: 875mps (2878fps)
EFFECTIVE RANGE: 800m (2624ft) plus
CYCLIC RATE OF FIRE: 600rpm

M14

The M14 was developed during the 1950s to use the standard 7.62mm NATO round. It was effectively the Garand rifle with a 20-round box magazine and a selective fire facility. Yet conversion was problematic and the production M14 only appeared in 1957. The M14 was reliable and hard-wearing, qualities it derived from its quality machining, which was more than needed to cope with the M14 when firing full auto, as the gun's weight and recoil made it difficult to control. Indeed, the M14 was not really suited to automatic fire; the barrel would quickly overheat and could not be changed when hot. Some models left out the automatic facility, although a bipod-fitted squad automatic, the M14A1, was developed in 1968. Despite this, the M14 has been popular, serving the US during the 1950s and 1960s. Production ended in 1964.

SPECIFICATIONS

COUNTRY OF ORIGIN: United States
CALIBRE: 7.62 x 51mm NATO
LENGTH: 1117mm (43.98in)
WEIGHT: 3.88kg (8.55lb)
BARREL: 558mm (21.97in), 4 grooves, rh
FEED: 20-round detachable box magazine
OPERATION: gas
MUZZLE VELOCITY: 595mps (1950fps)
EFFECTIVE RANGE: 800m (2624ft) plus
CYCLIC RATE OF FIRE: 750rpm

Beretta BM59

The BM59 grew out of the US M1 Garand rifle, which Beretta made in Italy following World War II. The redesign took place in 1959, when NATO members were standardising weapons to the 7.62mm calibre. The most fundamental differences were that the BM59 now had an extended 20-round magazine and it could be selected to fire full-auto. Minimal changes were made, and the M1's gas-operation system remained essentially the same. Once the BM59 was established, other models were brought out with varied butt, barrel, bayonet and grenade-launching adaptations for use by specialist units, such as airborne and mountain troops. A heavy barrelled version was also made for use in a sustained-fire role. The BM59 is now somewhat dated in weight and configuration.

SPECIFICATIONS

COUNTRY OF ORIGIN: Italy
CALIBRE: 7.62mm NATO
LENGTH: 1095mm (43.11in)
WEIGHT: 4.6kg (10.14lb)
BARREL: 490mm (19.29in), 4 grooves, rh
FEED: 20-round box
OPERATION: gas
MUZZLE VELOCITY: 823mps (2700fps)
EFFECTIVE RANGE: 800m (2624ft)
CYCLIC RATE OF FIRE: 750rpm

Kalashnikov AKM

While the original AK-47 was a superb gun in most respects, there were problems in the quality of its stamped steel receiver that let down its potentially good reliability. In 1951, the switch was made to a machined receiver, but this then made the gun's production cost per unit rise considerably. The solution was found in 1959 in the AKM (the M stands for 'Modernized'), the most prolific of the AK series, and the one most likely to be encountered when Kalashnikovs are present on the battlefield. It featured a higher quality stamped receiver ideal for the gun and it also took on several other minor improvements. These included an angled muzzle, which acted as a basic compensator to control muzzle climb, and a newly designed bayonet that could convert into a wire cutter. An AKM can usually be distinguished from an AK-47 by the recess above the magazine housing.

SPECIFICATIONS

COUNTRY OF ORIGIN: Soviet Union/Russia
CALIBRE: 7.62 x 39mm Soviet M1943
LENGTH: 880mm (34.65in)
WEIGHT: 4.3kg (9.48lb)
BARREL: 415mm (16.34in), 4 grooves, rh

FEED: 30-round detachable box magazine
OPERATION: gas
MUZZLE VELOCITY: 600mps (2350fps)
EFFECTIVE RANGE: 400m (1312ft)
CYCLIC RATE OF FIRE: 600rpm

Dragunov SVD

The Dragunov bears a family resemblance to the AK series of weapons, but it has been extensively re-engineered to meet the demands of the sniping role. It is semi-automatic, but the gas system works with a short-stroke piston, rather than the AK's long stroke to improve the weapon's stability. Accuracy comes from a combination of a very long barrel and the standard fitment of a PSO-1x4 telescopic sight, which can also act upon infra-red detections to give a night-sight capability. It has a first shot range of around 1000m (3280ft) and it is able to achieve this range by swapping the AK's 7.62mm Short cartridge for the older rimmed 7.62mm x 54R cartridge, the ancestry of which stretches back to the late 19th century. The overall result is a very capable sniper weapon that is both precise and rugged, and it has served well since it was introduced in 1963.

SPECIFICATIONS

COUNTRY OF ORIGIN: Soviet Union/Russia
CALIBRE: 7.62mm x 54R Soviet
LENGTH: 1225mm (48.20in)
WEIGHT: 4.31kg (9.50lb)
BARREL: 610mm (24.02in), 4 grooves, rh
FEED: 10-round detachable box magazine
OPERATION: gas
MUZZLE VELOCITY: 828mps (2720fps)
EFFECTIVE RANGE: 1000m (3280ft)
CYCLIC RATE OF FIRE: not applicable

Armalite AR-18

The AR-18 emerged from the Armalite factory in the mid-1960s in 5.56mm calibre, after a number of 7.62mm designs. The thinking behind the AR-18's design was to produce a simplified AR-15 (M16) for countries that needed something cheap to buy, easy to maintain and simple to manufacture. Although some resemblances remain between the AR-18 and the AR-15, the former gun had a different piston-driven gas operation and a much broader use of metal stamping and pressing. The whole gun breaks down into only a few parts and both sights were on a single section so that the zero was kept even after disassembly and reassembly. The AR-18, however, failed because of M16 domination, despite the fact that some suggest that this accurate and powerful weapon was actually the superior of the two.

SPECIFICATIONS

COUNTRY OF ORIGIN: United States
CALIBRE: 5.56mm M109
LENGTH: 965mm (37.99in) stock extended; 730mm (28.74in) stock folded
WEIGHT: 3.04kg (6.70lb)
BARREL: 463mm (18.25in), 4 grooves, rh
FEED: 20-round detachable box magazine
OPERATION: gas
MUZZLE VELOCITY: 990mps (2530fps)
EFFECTIVE RANGE: 500m (1640ft) plus
CYCLIC RATE OF FIRE: 750rpm

M16A1

Designed by Eugene Stoner, the M16 first appeared as the 7.62mm AR-10, followed by the AR-15, which was rechambered for the 5.56mm round. Licence to produce the AR-15 switched to Colt in 1959 and significant sales of the gun went out to Southeast Asia, the UK and the US Army, when it was retitled the M16. However, in early service in Vietnam, it had a tendency to jam and had to be kept very clean (not easy in the jungle). The problem was found to be a new propellant that caused excessive fouling; modifications to both gun and propellant left an excellent assault rifle, the M16A1. The plastic and pressed steel construction made it relatively light and the high-velocity of the round more than compensated for its small calibre in combat. The current standard M16 rifle is the M16A2.

SPECIFICATIONS

COUNTRY OF ORIGIN: United States
CALIBRE: 5.56 x 45mm M193
LENGTH: 990mm (38.98in)
WEIGHT: 2.86kg (6.31lb)
BARREL: 508mm (20in), 6 grooves, rh
FEED: 30-round detachable box magazine
OPERATION: gas
MUZZLE VELOCITY: 1000mps (3280fps)
EFFECTIVE RANGE: 500m (1640ft) plus
CYCLIC RATE OF FIRE: 800rpm

Heckler & Koch G3

Although the G3 does not have the fame of the M16 or the AK47, it still stands as one of the most widely distributed modern assault rifles, used by more than 50 international armies. Based on a CETME design, its operation is a roller-delayed blowback with a heritage that can be traced back to Mauser in the mid-1940s. The rugged operation makes the G3 an exceptionally dependable rifle in combat, firing the powerful 7.62mm NATO cartridge. Using the full-size rifle cartridge gave it great range and power, however, it also made it date quickly once the new 5.56mm weapons appeared on the scene. The gun could be rather heavy and had a crude appearance because of an extensive use of metal stampings. The G3 has been thoroughly combat-tested in theatres ranging from Africa and the Middle East to South America.

SPECIFICATIONS

COUNTRY OF ORIGIN: Germany
CALIBRE: 7.62mm NATO
LENGTH: 1025mm (40.35in)
WEIGHT: 4.4kg (9.70lb)
BARREL: 450mm (17.71in), 4 grooves, rh
FEED: 20-round detachable box magazine
OPERATION: delayed blowback
MUZZLE VELOCITY: 800mps (2625fps)
EFFECTIVE RANGE: 500m (1640ft) plus
CYCLIC RATE OF FIRE: 500–600rpm

Heckler & Koch HK13E

After Heckler & Koch produced the 5.56m HK33 assault rifle in the 1970s, the company designed a new light machine gun as its partner for use as a squad support weapon. This was the HK13, which fired the same calibre round as the HK33, but from a heavier, quick-change barrel. As such it was little different to the rifle, and there soon emerged the need for some modifications. The result was the HK13E. Improvements included a longer receiver, which imparted a less severe recoil, a three-round burst facility and the option of switching between magazine and belt feed with a fairly easy conversion. The furniture was also enhanced to give greater versatility to the gun. A forward grip was fitted for use when firing from the hip and also to allow the rapid change of the barrel when necessary.

SPECIFICATIONS

COUNTRY OF ORIGIN: Germany
CALIBRE: 5.56 x 45mm NATO
LENGTH: 1030mm (40.55in)
WEIGHT: 8kg (17.64lb)
BARREL: 450mm (17.72in), 6 grooves, rh
FEED: 20- or 30-round detachable box or belt feed
OPERATION: roller-locked delayed blowback, air-cooled
MUZZLE VELOCITY: 925mps (3035fps)
EFFECTIVE RANGE: 1000m (3280ft) plus
CYCLIC RATE OF FIRE: 750rpm

Heckler & Koch G3SG1

The G3 has many variants, including a version in 5.56mm calibre, the HK 33 – which at one stage looked like being adopted by the German Army as their standard rifle – and folding stock models. It also came in its own sniper version known as the Scharfschützen Gewehr, or SG-1. This was essentially a standard G3 rifle, but featured a telescopic sight (usually a Schmidt & Bender) and also a more sensitive trigger unit and specially selected barrel. It has a lightweight bipod attached to the front of the foregrip. In this form the G3 entered service as a police weapon. The rifle itself is identical to the G3, using a minimum of expensive machined parts and, like the Lee Enfield Enforcers in British police service, continues to give good results due to the rugged nature of the design, which can withstand rough treatment.

SPECIFICATIONS
COUNTRY OF ORIGIN: Germany
CALIBRE: 7.62 x 51mm NATO
LENGTH: 1025mm (40.35in)
WEIGHT: 4.4kg (9.70lb)
BARREL: 450mm (17.71in), 4 grooves, rh
FEED: 20-round detachable box magazine
OPERATION: delayed blowback
MUZZLE VELOCITY: 800mps (2625fps)
EFFECTIVE RANGE: 500m (1640ft) plus
CYCLIC RATE OF FIRE: 500–600rpm

M21 Rifle

Although the 7.62mm M14 rifle was superseded by the new high-velocity 5.56mm guns, it lived on in several new incarnations. In particular, the US forces retained it as a sniping rifle (the 7.62mm round being more effective for sniping) designated the Rifle 7.62mm M14 National Match (Accurized), which became known simply as the M21. The most obvious difference between the M21 and the standard M14 is the x 3 Leatherwood Redfield telescopic sight. Less apparent are improvements in the barrel, trigger and gas operation, which are manufactured to much higher standards and tolerances. The barrel is left without the usual chromium plating to avoid manufacturing errors. The M21 has proved to be a very capable sniper rifle and has been used outside the US by forces such as the Israel Defense Forces.

SPECIFICATIONS

COUNTRY OF ORIGIN: United States
CALIBRE: 7.62 x 51mm NATO
LENGTH: 1120mm (44.09in)
WEIGHT: 5.55kg (12.24lb) loaded
BARREL: 559mm (22in), 4 grooves, rh
FEED: 20-round detachable box magazine
OPERATION: gas, self-loading
MUZZLE VELOCITY: 853mps (2798fps)
EFFECTIVE RANGE: 800m (2624ft) plus
CYCLIC RATE OF FIRE: semi-automatic

Beretta AR70/90

The AR70/90 was developed during the 1980s and brought into production in 1990 as a much improved, more reliable version of its predecessor, the AR70/223. The AR70/90 takes on board the full spectrum of capabilities demanded of a modern assault rifle. It can fire in semi- and full-automatic modes and three-round bursts, and its variant models alter barrel length and stock configuration (folding or fixed) according to usage. The SCS-70/90 model has a folding butt and 320mm (12.5in) barrel. It accepts standard M16 magazines and has a carrying handle/sight situated above the receiver. The AR70/90 also accepts a bipod for roles of infantry support. It is currently used by the Italian Army.

SPECIFICATIONS

COUNTRY OF ORIGIN: Italy
CALIBRE: 5.56mm NATO
LENGTH: 998mm (39.29in)
WEIGHT: 3.99kg (8.79lb)
BARREL: 450mm (17.72in), 6 grooves, rh
FEED: 20- or 30-round box magazine
OPERATION: gas, self-loading
MUZZLE VELOCITY: 950mps (3116fps)
EFFECTIVE RANGE: 500m (1640ft)
CYCLIC RATE OF FIRE: 650rpm

Galil ARM

The Galil was designed as a lighter replacement for the FN FAL rifle for the Israel Defense Forces (IDF) in the wake of the 1967 Six-Day War. After an intense period of study of the world's assault rifles, Israeli Military Industries (IMI) opted for a version of the AK-series rotating-bolt action and the Galil was initially built using the body of another AK derivative, the Finnish M62 Valmet. The standard rifle is the Galil ARM, which is fitted with a bipod and carrying handle, and can be used in a light machine-gun role; the Galil AR lacks both bipod and carrying handle, and the Galil SAR (Short Assault Rifle) is the same as the AR, but with a shorter barrel. An excellent gun; a version of the Galil was made for 7.62mm calibre, but the 5.56mm version is dominant in Israel and other international armies. All Galils come with either folding or fixed butts.

SPECIFICATIONS

COUNTRY OF ORIGIN: Israel
CALIBRE: 5.56mm NATO
LENGTH: 979mm (38.54in) overall; 742mm (29.21in) stock folded
WEIGHT: 4.35kg (9.59lb)
BARREL: 460mm (18.11in), 6 grooves, rh
FEED: 35- or 50-round box magazine
OPERATION: gas, self-loading
MUZZLE VELOCITY: 990mps (3250fps)
EFFECTIVE RANGE: 800m (2624ft) plus
CYCLIC RATE OF FIRE: 650rpm

Galil Sniper

The Galil Sniper rifle emerged as a redesign by Israel Military Industries (IMI) of the standard Galil service rifle, but that redesign has been exceptionally thorough. In addition to a heavy barrel and bipod, the Galil Sniper differs from the service gun by having an adjustable stock (with shoulder and cheek adjustments) that folds down for storage, a muzzle brake to limit recoil and a Nimrod x 6 telescopic sight (fitted to the left side of the receiver). In addition, almost all the internal workings have been exhaustively retuned for the gun's accurate role and the weapon is only capable of semi-automatic fire. Having been born from the service rifle has also ensured that the gun is robust enough to handle military life. In both trials and combat, the Galil sniper has shown its lethal accuracy up to, and beyond, ranges of 800m (2624ft).

SPECIFICATIONS

COUNTRY OF ORIGIN: Israel
CALIBRE: 7.62mm NATO
LENGTH: 1115mm (43.89in) stock extended; 840mm (33.07in) stock folded
WEIGHT: 6.4kg (14.11lb)
BARREL: 508mm (20in) without muzzle brake, 4 grooves, rh
FEED: 20-round box magazine
OPERATION: gas, self-loading
MUZZLE VELOCITY: 815mps (2675fps)
EFFECTIVE RANGE: 800m (2624ft) plus
CYCLIC RATE OF FIRE: not applicable

Ruger Mini-14

A quick glance at the Ruger Mini-14 shows that it is a more compact version of the M14 rifle, which in turn derives from the M1 Garand, the standard US rifle of World War II. Like both of those weapons, the Mini-14 works on a gas-operated rotating-bolt system, but it is calibrated for the high-velocity (but lighter weight) 5.56mm NATO or M193 rounds. Although the recoil of this round is less than the 7.62mm rounds of the M14, the gas pressure was still high enough to warrant some re-engineering. Thus, the gas piston is driven only a short distance via pressure on its cup head before the gas is vented out through an aperture and the piston carries the bolt back under its own momentum. The lightweight controllability of the Mini-14 has allowed its use by civilian, military and police customers, where it has proved popular.

SPECIFICATIONS

COUNTRY OF ORIGIN: United States
CALIBRE: 5.56mm NATO or M193
LENGTH: 946mm (37.24in)
WEIGHT: 2.9kg (6.70lb)
BARREL: 470mm (18.50in), 6 grooves, rh
FEED: 5-, 10-, 20- or 30-round detachable box magazine
OPERATION: gas
MUZZLE VELOCITY: 1005mps (3297fps)
EFFECTIVE RANGE: 400m (1312ft)
CYCLIC RATE OF FIRE: 750rpm

Heckler & Koch PSG 1

The Heckler & Koch G3 rifle has already spawned two sniper weapons – the Heckler & Koch G3 A3ZF and the G3 SG/1 – which are only marginally different from the standard gun. The PSG 1 (Präzisionsschützengewehr, or High Precision Rifle) features the G3's roller-locked delayed blowback system; however, it is actually a complete reworking of the G3 design for precision sniping. The barrel itself is a meticulous heavy-duty and extra-long affair featuring a polygonal-rifled bore. This, when used in tandem with the PSG 1's 6 x 42 telescopic sight, which features illuminated cross hairs, gives superb accuracy up to 600m (1969ft), the sight's maximum range configuration with the lowest of its six settings being 100m (328ft). The PSG 1 stock and cheek rest are adjustable in both length and height, and the model can also be fitted with a lightweight bipod.

SPECIFICATIONS

COUNTRY OF ORIGIN: Germany
CALIBRE: 7.62 x 51mm NATO
LENGTH: 1208mm (47.56in)
WEIGHT: 8.1kg (17.86lb)
BARREL: 650mm (25.59in), 4 grooves, rh
FEED: 5- or 20-round detachable box magazine
OPERATION: roller-locked delayed blowback
MUZZLE VELOCITY: 815mps (2675fps)
EFFECTIVE RANGE: 600m (1969ft)
CYCLIC RATE OF FIRE: semi-automatic

FN FNC

The Fabrique Nationale FNC was based on the FN CAL (Carabine, Automatic, Legère), a 5.56mm update of the famous FN FAL rifle that had sold so well for the company. The FN CAL had been somewhat ahead of its time in calibre and features, and so was relatively unsuccessful, but the FN FNC was produced when the small-calibre, high-velocity rifle became more in vogue. The FNC found greater market success because – through the use of alloys, plastics, stampings and pressings – it was cheaper to manufacture than the CAL, and it could also meet with the ever-growing needs of standardization by accepting the ubiquitous US M16 magazine. Use of the FNC has spread across the world since its appearance, particularly centred in countries such as Sweden (who designate it the AK5), Belgium and Indonesia (where it is manufactured under licence).

SPECIFICATIONS
COUNTRY OF ORIGIN: Belgium
CALIBRE: 5.56 x 45mm NATO
LENGTH: 997mm (39.25in) stock extended; 766mm (30.15in) stock folded
WEIGHT: 3.8kg (8.38lb)
BARREL: 449mm (17.68in), 6 grooves, rh
FEED: 30-round detachable box magazine
OPERATION: gas
MUZZLE VELOCITY: 965mps (3165fps)
EFFECTIVE RANGE: 500m (1640ft) plus
CYCLIC RATE OF FIRE: 600–750rpm

Valmet M76

The Valmet M76 is of Soviet AK-47 derivation, but takes advantage of new materials and manufacturing processes, as well as improving on some of the AK-47's strengths. The furniture is the most updated feature of the weapon. The butt comes in a variety of fixed or folding configurations, most particularly a tubular steel variety (the M76T); it also comes in plastic or wooden materials to save weight. At the front of the gun is a plastic forestock and the trigger unit is detachable so that the gun can be fired by a user wearing bulky Arctic mittens, an essential feature for the local climate. A squad automatic version of the M76, the M78, has also been produced, which features a bipod and heavy barrel for light-support fire roles. Being closely derived from the AK weapons, the M76 is a predictably rugged and dependable gun and is capable of hard use.

SPECIFICATIONS

COUNTRY OF ORIGIN: Finland
CALIBRE: 7.62 x 39mm Soviet M43; 5.56 x 45mm
LENGTH: 914mm (35.98in)
WEIGHT: 3.6kg (7.94lb)
BARREL: 420mm (16.53in), 4 grooves, rh
FEED: 15-, 20- or 30-round detachable box magazine
OPERATION: gas
MUZZLE VELOCITY: 720mps (2362fps)
EFFECTIVE RANGE: 500m (1640ft) plus
CYCLIC RATE OF FIRE: 650rpm

SIG SG540

The SG540 has become a broad export for the Swiss firm SIG, going out to markets across the world (particularly those in Africa, South America and the Middle East) and being manufactured for a short time under licence by Manurhin of France. The gun is a rotating-bolt gas-operated weapon, which had its ancestry back in the Stgw 57 assault rifle. It is 5.56mm in calibre along with the SG543; the SG542 was made for the 7.62 x 51mm NATO round. Its greatest virtues are its reliability and adaptability through a range of different fittings. A bipod and telescopic sight can make it into an effective sniper rifle, while the flash-compensator doubles as a grenade-launching mount. The SG540 also features a tilted drum rear sight, which can give various range settings at 100m (328ft) intervals. Overall, the SG540 is an excellent infantry weapon of its type.

SPECIFICATIONS

COUNTRY OF ORIGIN: Switzerland
CALIBRE: 5.56 x 45mm NATO
LENGTH: 950mm (37.40in)
WEIGHT: 3.26kg (7.19lb)
BARREL: 460mm (18.11in), 6 grooves, rh
FEED: 20- or 30-round detachable box magazine
OPERATION: gas, rotating bolt
MUZZLE VELOCITY: 980mps (3215fps); 5.56mm
EFFECTIVE RANGE: 800m (2624ft)
CYCLIC RATE OF FIRE: 650–800rpm

Kalashnikov AK-74

The AK-74 is now the standard rifle of the Russian armed forces and it began its replacement of the AKM rifle during the late 1970s. To all intents and purposes, it is the 7.62mm AKM rifle rechambered and modified for the smaller 5.45mm cartridge, part of the worldwide trend for smaller calibre, high-velocity weapons that occurred during the 1960s and 1970s, although the West opted for the 5.56mm round. To compensate for the small calibre, the round itself is steel cored and hollow tipped, with a rearward centre of gravity, the result being that the bullet tumbles through the target on impact, causing far greater damage to a body than a 'clean' bullet entry, an effect outlawed by many nations. The distinguishing feature of the AK-74 is the large muzzle brake, which, combined with the round, means that the gun produces almost no recoil.

SPECIFICATIONS

COUNTRY OF ORIGIN: Soviet Union/Russia
CALIBRE: 5.45mm M74
LENGTH: 940mm (37in) stock extended
WEIGHT: 3.6kg (7.94lb)
BARREL: 400mm (15.75in), 4 grooves, rh
FEED: 30-round box
OPERATION: gas
MUZZLE VELOCITY: 900mps (2952fps)
EFFECTIVE RANGE: 300m (984ft)
CYCLIC RATE OF FIRE: 650rpm

Kalashnikov AKS-74

Issued at the same time as its fixed stock counterpart, the AKS-74 is little different from the standard AK-74 rifle. In fact the only change is the use of the tubular folding stock. This folds to the left of the rifle's body, in contrast to the earlier AK-series folding stock models, whose stock would sit under the rifle when not in use. Another version of the rifle, the AK-74M, is also fitted with a folding stock, but this is a solid plastic version, which folds to the right of the receiver. All the AK-74 series rifles are fitted with the recoil-reducing muzzle brake, which follows the Soviet doctrine of preferring troops to produce grouped automatic suppressive fire rather than aimed shots. One of the drawbacks of the muzzle brake, however, is that it does not reduce muzzle flash, which is approximately three times normal. The AK-74 series is licence-produced in Bulgaria, Hungary, Poland and Romania.

SPECIFICATIONS

COUNTRY OF ORIGIN: Soviet Union/Russia
CALIBRE: 5.45mm M74
LENGTH: 690mm (27.17in) stock folded
WEIGHT: 3.6kg (7.94lb)
BARREL: 400mm (15.75in), 4 grooves, rh
FEED: 30-round box
OPERATION: gas
MUZZLE VELOCITY: 900mps (2952fps)
EFFECTIVE RANGE: 300m (984ft)
CYCLIC RATE OF FIRE: 650rpm

Kalashnikov AKSU-74

This short, powerful weapon is essentially a compressed version of the AKS-74 assault rifle. It has little to distinguish it from that gun except for the dramatically shortened barrel and gas tube, and the flared muzzle attachment, which hides some of the flash and controls some of the recoil from the rifle-calibre round. The AKSU-74's original customers were reportedly Soviet special forces – indeed, the first use of the gun was in Afghanistan in 1982 – and also armoured vehicle personnel who needed a short weapon to store in their vehicles. This storage would have been made easier by the metal stock, which lays alongside the receiver when folded. Whoever the intended users, the AKSU-74's distribution seems to have widened to general troops.

SPECIFICATIONS

COUNTRY OF ORIGIN: Soviet Union/Russia
CALIBRE: 5.45mm M74
LENGTH: 750mm (29.53in) stock extended; 527mm (20.75in) stock folded
WEIGHT: 3.4kg (7.49lb)
BARREL: 269mm (10.59in), 4 grooves, rh
FEED: 30-round detachable box magazine
OPERATION: blowback
MUZZLE VELOCITY: 488mps (1600fps)
EFFECTIVE RANGE: 250m (820ft)
CYCLIC RATE OF FIRE: 700rpm

Steyr-Mannlicher AUG

The bullpup-design Steyr-Mannlicher Armee Universal Gewehr (AUG) is one of the best assault rifles in existence today. Its rather fragile appearance masks an unswerving reliability under the hardest conditions, and it is very stable and accurate. Its weight is kept down by an extensive use of advanced plastics, even in areas such as the firing mechanism and its clear-plastic magazine, which allows the user to check ammunition usage. Fire selection is accomplished by a two-stage trigger and the firing mechanism is easily changed to vary the selective-fire configuration. Indeed, the whole rifle is modular in form, with short and long barrels that are interchangeable through a simple twist of the front grip. Standard in the Austrian Army, the AUG is spreading throughout the world in places such as Australia and the US.

SPECIFICATIONS

COUNTRY OF ORIGIN: Austria
CALIBRE: 5.56 x 45mm M198 or NATO
LENGTH: 790mm (31.10in)
WEIGHT: 3.6kg (7.93lb)
BARREL: 508mm (20in), 6 grooves, rh
FEED: 30- or 42-round detachable box magazine
OPERATION: gas
MUZZLE VELOCITY: 970mps (3182fps)
EFFECTIVE RANGE: 500m (1640ft) plus
CYCLIC RATE OF FIRE: 650rpm

FAMAS

The FAMAS is now the French forces' standard side arm and it is an all-round excellent weapon. Firing standard NATO and French Service 5.56mm ammunition, its bullpup design (with the chamber behind the trigger) gives it good accuracy over 400m (1312ft) due to the length of its barrel. Its light delayed-blowback operation, which uses a two-part bolt, permits a very high rate of fire – 900rpm can empty the magazine in seconds – something which the trigger's lightness does nothing to control. The FAMAS started to enter French service in the early 1980s and it has given French troops a world-class firearm. The latest model, the F2, has dispensed with the trigger guard in favour of a full handguard – ideal for use with gloved hands – and it will also take the M16 magazine, now almost an essential feature of NATO weapons.

SPECIFICATIONS

COUNTRY OF ORIGIN: France
CALIBRE: 5.56mm NATO or Type France
LENGTH: 757mm (29.80in)
WEIGHT: 3.61kg (7.96lb)
BARREL: 488mm (19.21in), 3 grooves, rh
FEED: 25-round detachable box magazine
OPERATION: gas
MUZZLE VELOCITY: 960mps (3150fps)
EFFECTIVE RANGE: 400m (1312ft)
CYCLIC RATE OF FIRE: 900–1000rpm

Vektor R4

The Vektor R4 is a superb assault rifle based on the Israeli Galil and one that acted as a replacement for the South African Defence Force's FN FALs and Heckler & Koch G3s. The R4 makes greater use of a high-impact nylon/ glass fibre mix in its construction than the Galil and is generally stronger and larger than the Israeli gun, although it weighs approximately the same. A bipod fitting comes as standard for the rifle, which also has a wire-cutting feature and a bottle-opener (the latter prevents soldiers opening bottles on precision gun components, such as the magazine receiver lips, and thus damaging them). A further feature is the use of tritium inserts into the sights for night firing. The R4 is at the top of a series of weapons, which includes a carbine version, the R5 and the even shorter R6, with its 280mm (1.10in) barrel.

SPECIFICATIONS
COUNTRY OF ORIGIN: South Africa
CALIBRE: 5.56 x 45mm M193
LENGTH: 1005mm (35.97in) stock extended; 740mm (29.13in) stock folded
WEIGHT: 4.3kg (9.48lb)
BARREL: 460mm (18.11in), 6 grooves, rh
FEED: 35 or 50-round detachable box magazine
OPERATION: gas
MUZZLE VELOCITY: 980mps (3215fps)
EFFECTIVE RANGE: 500m (1640ft) plus
CYCLIC RATE OF FIRE: 650rpm

Walther WA2000

The Walther WA2000 represents a revolution in sniper weapon design. The barrel is clamped at the front and rear so that it does not twist on firing, while the rest of the barrel is free from any contact with furniture to prevent further distortions or movement disturbing the gun's aim. Furthermore, the barrel is fluted to dampen vibrations and aid cooling. The barrel is set in line with the user's shoulder to reduce recoil and the bolt mechanism sits behind the handgrip in a bullpup arrangement. All stock furniture is fully adjustable and, when firing the .300 Winchester Magnum and using the standard Schmidt and Bender x 2.5 to x 10 sight, the rifle's accuracy is considerable. However, its sophistication and price tag mean that it is more suited to police and security operations than arduous military use in the field.

SPECIFICATIONS

COUNTRY OF ORIGIN: Germany
CALIBRE: .300 Winchester Magnum
LENGTH: 905mm (35.63in)
WEIGHT: 8.31kg (18.32lb) loaded, with telescopic sight
BARREL: 650mm (25.59in)
FEED: 6-round detachable box magazine
OPERATION: gas
MUZZLE VELOCITY: c.800mps (2624fps)
EFFECTIVE RANGE: 1000m (3280ft) plus
CYCLIC RATE OF FIRE: not applicable

SAR 80

The SAR 80 was inspired by the US M16 rifle, but, following an intense design liaison between Chartered Industries of Singapore and Sterling Armaments of England, a weapon perhaps even superior to the M16 was born. Like the M16, it is a gas-operated weapon using a straight-in-line design to aid controllability and accuracy, and it can accept the standard 5.56mm M16 magazine. Singapore's investment in new technology, however, has made the SAR 80 a much cheaper weapon to manufacture and orders are already spreading across the world (large numbers were seen in Yugoslavia during the civil war.) The SAR 80 can give single, three-round burst or full-automatic fire, and also accepts rifle grenades directly onto its flash-suppressor. These features plus its overall quality mean that the SAR 80 seems destined to be one of Singapore's successful exports.

SPECIFICATIONS

COUNTRY OF ORIGIN: Singapore
CALIBRE: 5.56 x 45mm NATO
LENGTH: 970mm (38.18in)
WEIGHT: 3.17kg (7lb)
BARREL: 459mm (18.07in), 6 grooves, rh
FEED: 30-round detachable box magazine
OPERATION: gas, self-loading
MUZZLE VELOCITY: 970mps (3182fps)
EFFECTIVE RANGE: 800m (2600ft) plus
CYCLIC RATE OF FIRE: 700rpm

Beretta SC70

The SC70 was a carbine variant of the AR70, designed for greater portability and use within confined areas such as buildings and vehicles. In most respects it is little different to the standard rifle, except that it had a folding metal butt stock that could be collapsed for ease of storage when required. With the butt folded, the overall length of the gun was taken down to 736mm (28.97in). The SC70 also led to a weapon, the SC70 Short, which had the main dimensions reduced, in a similar way to the Soviet AKSU-74. The SC70 Short had a 320mm (12.59in) barrel, which reduced its overall accuracy but, combined with the folding metal stock, made the gun very convenient for use on covert or security operations when a weapon had to have limited visible presence.

SPECIFICATIONS

COUNTRY OF ORIGIN: Italy
CALIBRE: 5.56 x 45mm NATO
LENGTH: 960mm (37.79in) stock extended; 736mm (28.97in) stock folded
WEIGHT: 3.8kg (8.37lb)
BARREL: 452mm (17.79in)
FEED: 30-round detachable box magazine
OPERATION: gas
MUZZLE VELOCITY: 962mps (3180fps)
EFFECTIVE RANGE: 800m (2624ft)
CYCLIC RATE OF FIRE: 630rpm

Barrett Light Fifty M82A1

The Barrett Light Fifty M82A1 is a truly fearsome sniper weapon, firing a .50in Browning Machine Gun (BMG) round over distances of up to and over a mile. The destructive force of the .50in round makes it decisive in both anti-personnel and anti-materiel roles. A semi-automatic, short-recoil weapon working off an 11-round box magazine; the Barrett controls its recoil mainly through a large muzzle brake, which diverts some 30 per cent of its gases out at right angles to the direction of the barrel. The highly specialist nature of the weapon has somewhat limited its use and it is almost entirely in the hands of US special forces, although some have even turned up in terrorist use in Northern Ireland. It also saw service in the Gulf, where it proved a useful weapon over long ranges. It was, however, not the only .50in sniper rifle on the market and production of this particular weapon ceased in 1992.

SPECIFICATIONS
COUNTRY OF ORIGIN: United States
CALIBRE: .50in BMG
LENGTH: 1549mm (60.98in)
WEIGHT: 14.7kg (32.41lb)
BARREL: 838mm (32.99in), 8 grooves, rh
FEED: 11-round box magazine
OPERATION: short-recoil, semi-automatic
MUZZLE VELOCITY: 843mps (2800fps)
EFFECTIVE RANGE: 1000m (3280ft) plus
CYCLIC RATE OF FIRE: not applicable

Enfield L85A1 (SA80)

The L85A1 (otherwise known as the SA80) is one of those firearms which is sound in theory and practice, but which has been badly let down in active-service conditions. Built by the Royal Small Arms Factory, it replaced the L1A1 Self-Loading Rifle (the British variant of the FN FAL rifle) as the British Army's standard infantry weapon in the early 1980s. Gas-operated and working on a 'bullpup' design, which places the magazine behind the trigger (thus maximiZing barrel length), the L85A1 is accurate and has very little recoil. First-line troops have the weapon fitted with SUSAT (Sight Unit, Small Arm, Trilux) optical sight, which further enhances the accuracy of use. However, its undoubtedly fine design qualities are let down by both engineering defects in the early models and a lack of durability under even moderately dirty conditions.

SPECIFICATIONS

COUNTRY OF ORIGIN: United Kingdom
CALIBRE: 5.56mm NATO
LENGTH: 785mm (30.90in)
WEIGHT: 3.80kg (8.37lb)
BARREL: 518mm (20.39in), 6 grooves, rh
FEED: 30-round detachable box magazine
OPERATION: gas
MUZZLE VELOCITY: 940mps (3084fps)
EFFECTIVE RANGE: 400m (1312ft)
CYCLIC RATE OF FIRE: 700rpm

L85A1 Carbine

The standard issue L85A1 has yet to prove itself as a competent weapon for combat use, so the carbine version will probably not reach more successful distribution until questions about its parent weapon are answered. The thinking behind the carbine version is that of all carbines, a shorter weapon that will be of use to either soldiers in cramped storage conditions such as tanks and APVs, or a weapon ideal for use by special forces or troops on covert operations. In terms of an on-paper comparison, the L85A1 carbine is little different from the standard rifle except in terms of dimensions, but with 76mm (2.99in) taken off the barrel length, the effective range has also been slightly compressed. The weight and length reductions on the carbine make it a very compact weapon, especially as the original rifle is fairly short to begin with.

SPECIFICATIONS
COUNTRY OF ORIGIN: United Kingdom
CALIBRE: 5.56 x 45mm NATO
LENGTH: 709mm (27.91in)
WEIGHT: 3.71kg (8.18lb)
BARREL: 442mm (17.40in)
FEED: 30-round detachable box magazine
OPERATION: gas
MUZZLE VELOCITY: 940mps (3084fps)
EFFECTIVE RANGE: 300m (984ft)
CYCLIC RATE OF FIRE: 700rpm

Light Support Weapon L86A1

The introduction of the 5.56mm L85A1 as the standard British Army assault rifle meant that a new support weapon had to be developed with the same calibre. The result was the L86A1 Light Support Weapon (LSW), essentially the same weapon as the rifle, but with a heavier and longer barrel and a rear grip to aid sustained fire. The bolt system, however, is different in that it stays open when the trigger is released to allow barrel cooling. This is essential as there is no quick-change barrel, so the gun must be fired in controlled bursts with adequate time for cooling. The range of the LSW is only marginally better than the L85A1, but its accuracy is considerable; even when fitted with the standard SUSAT (Sight Unit, Small Arms Trilux) sight, it can still be used as a single-shot sniper weapon.

SPECIFICATIONS

COUNTRY OF ORIGIN: United Kingdom
CALIBRE: 5.56 x 45mm NATO
LENGTH: 900mm (35.43in)
WEIGHT: 5.4kg (11.90lb)
BARREL: 646mm (25.43in), 6 grooves, rh
FEED: 30-round box magazine
OPERATION: gas, air-cooled
MUZZLE VELOCITY: 970mps (3182fps)
EFFECTIVE RANGE: 1000m (3280ft)
CYCLIC RATE OF FIRE: 700rpm

Heckler & Koch G11

The Hecker & Koch G11 gives us a glimpse of the future of individual weaponry. It fires caseless rounds that consist of rectangular blocks of propellant with the bullet and percussion cap set in. Advantages include reduced cost and weight, no ejection and extraction stoppages, more economical production and smaller cartridge dimensions.

The rounds are fed from a horizontal magazine attached above the barrel. In full automatic mode, 600rpm is achieved; in three-round burst, this figure climbs to 2200rpm, due to all three rounds being fired in one cycle. The three-round speed enables great accuracy with climb almost eliminated. The G11 was intended as the German Army's standard rifle replacement in 1990, but internal disputes have kept it the preserve of special forces.

SPECIFICATIONS

COUNTRY OF ORIGIN: Germany
CALIBRE: 4.7 x 33mm DM11 caseless
LENGTH: 752.5mm (29.62in)
WEIGHT: 3.80kg (8.38lb)
BARREL: 537.5mm (21.16in), 6 grooves, polygonal, rh
FEED: 50-round detachable box magazine
OPERATION: gas
MUZZLE VELOCITY: 930mps (3050fps)
EFFECTIVE RANGE: 500m (1640ft) plus
CYCLIC RATE OF FIRE: 600rpm (full automatic);
2200rpm (three-round burst)

Kalashnikov AK-103

The AKs are the most widely produced and distributed firearms in history. The series started with the AK-47, developed just after World War II, to provide an infantry weapon that was both resilient and fast-firing. Part of Mikhail Kalashnikov's inspiration was the German MP44 and its use of the new 7.92mm *kurz* cartridge. The AK-47 was a simple gas-operated design using a rotating bolt. It had a chromium-plated barrel and generally high-quality machining and finishing. It took until 1959 to perfect the design and production process, but once this had been achieved, the Soviets were left with a truly seminal firearm. It could operate under the harshest of conditions without malfunction, was easily maintained and could compete with any Western firearm. It was also capable of extremely swift production and use of the AK-47 spread around the globe.

SPECIFICATIONS

COUNTRY OF ORIGIN: Soviet Union/Russia
CALIBRE: 7.62 x 39mm Soviet M1943
LENGTH: 880mm (34.65in)
WEIGHT: 4.3kg (9.48lb)
BARREL: 415mm (16.34in), 4 grooves, rh
FEED: 30-round detachable box magazine
OPERATION: gas
MUZZLE VELOCITY: 600mps (2350fps)
EFFECTIVE RANGE: 400m (1312ft)
CYCLIC RATE OF FIRE: 600rpm

FN F2000

The FN F2000 is one of a new generation of assault rifles. Firing standard 5.56 x45mm NATO rounds, it has a compact bullpup layout and a gas-operated, rotating-bolt (seven lugs) operating mechanism. One distinctive feature is the front ejection system; the spent cartridge cases are redirected from the chamber to an ejection port near the muzzle. This configuration aids accurate shooting (the shooter doesn't have to cope with hot cases ejecting close to his face) and makes the weapon ideally suited to firing through vehicle ports. Other virtues of the FN F2000 are its completely ambidextrous layout and its modularity; it can take numerous add-ons, from optical sights and laser rangefinders through to 40mm grenade launchers and riot-control weapons. Currently it has few buyers, but as its qualities become more widely known this situation is likely to change.

SPECIFICATIONS

COUNTRY OF ORIGIN: Belgium
CALIBRE: 5.56 x 45mm NATO
LENGTH: 694mm (27.32in)
WEIGHT: 3.6kg (7.93lb) empty, standard configuration
BARREL: 400mm (15.75in)
FEED: 30-round detachable box magazine
OPERATION: gas
MUZZLE VELOCITY: 900mps (2953fps)
EFFECTIVE RANGE: 500m (1640ft)
CYCLIC RATE OF FIRE: 850rpm

AN-94

The AN-94 'Abakan' was developed during the late 1980s and early 1990s as a replacement for the 5.45 x 39mm AN-74 series of rifles in Russian service. It is a technologically complex and innovative weapon. Although gas-operated, it uses a system labelled 'blowback shifted pulse', which is capable of delivering a two-round burst (the rifle's standard burst setting) at a rate of 1800rpm, the user essentially feeling one recoil impulse for the two shots, thereby improving accuracy. When fired on full-auto, the first two shots are at this higher rate, before settling down to a cyclical rate of 600rpm. The cost of this ability is a complicated internal mechanism, which sacrifices the simplicity of the traditional AK model. The Abakan can take standard 30- or 45-round AK-74 magazines or new 60-round boxes, and includes an advanced five-aperture rear sighting system.

SPECIFICATIONS

COUNTRY OF ORIGIN: Russia/CIS
CALIBRE: 5.45 x 39mm
LENGTH: 943mm (37.13in)
WEIGHT: 3.85kg (8.49lb)
BARREL: 520mm (20.47in)
FEED: 30-round detachable box magazine
OPERATION: gas, rotating bolt
MUZZLE VELOCITY: not available
EFFECTIVE RANGE: 500m (1640ft)
CYCLIC RATE OF FIRE: 600rpm

M4

Although carbine versions of the AR15/M16 family have been around since the 1970s, the M4 was taken into US military service in the 1990s, essentially as a replacement for various pistols and submachine-guns that had fallen out of service. Yet it has also been adopted by many soldiers as a straightforward replacement for the much longer M16 rifles, being compact and easy to handle in urban warfare scenarios. It has a shortened barrel and a four-position sliding buttstock, the latter enabling the firearm to be adapted to a soldier's personal dimensions. In most other regards, including the 5.56 x 45mm calibre and the direct impingement gas-operating system, the weapon is the same as its larger brethren. One point of controversy is that some firearms experts claim that the shorter barrel of the M4 reduces the efficacy of the 5.56mm bullet in terms of its take-down power, on account of reduced muzzle velocity.

SPECIFICATIONS

COUNTRY OF ORIGIN: United States
CALIBRE: 5.56 x 45mm NATO
LENGTH: 840mm (33.07in) stock extended
WEIGHT: 2.79kg (6.15lb)
BARREL: 370mm (14.57in)

FEED: 30-round detachable box magazine
OPERATION: gas
MUZZLE VELOCITY: 884mps (2900fps)
EFFECTIVE RANGE: 600m (1969ft)
CYCLIC RATE OF FIRE: 700–950rpm

QBZ-95

Having lagged behind the rest of the world in terms of assault rifle design, in the 1990s, China revealed the QBZ-95 as a new generation of infantry firepower. The impetus behind the rifle was the development of a 5.8 x 42mm cartridge during the late 1980s, which Chinese designers claimed had superior performance to its Western rival, the 5.56 x 45mm NATO. The QBZ-95 was one of a family of weapons created to take the new cartridge. It is of bullpup layout and is a gas-operated, rotating-bolt rifle. The carrying handle at the top of the gun also incorporates an integral rear sight, although the gun can also take external optical or night-vision sights. Underbelly fitment includes a bayonet or a grenade launcher. Other members of the family include sniper, carbine and light support (bipod-mounted) weapons.

SPECIFICATIONS

COUNTRY OF ORIGIN: China
CALIBRE: 5.8 x 42mm
LENGTH: 760mm (29.92in)
WEIGHT: 3.4kg (749lb)
BARREL: 520mm (20.47in)
FEED: 30-round detachable box magazine
OPERATION: gas, rotating bolt
MUZZLE VELOCITY: n/a
EFFECTIVE RANGE: 500m (1640ft)
CYCLIC RATE OF FIRE: 650rpm

Heckler & Koch G36

The G36 was a development intended to take over from the HK33 assault rifle. It was unveiled in 1997, and in it, Heckler & Koch have moved away from the roller-locked delayed blowback operation of their previous assault rifles to a gas-operated system of a type similar to that used in the Armalite AR-18. The G36 comes in three versions: a standard G36 rifle with bipod, the G36K carbine with more compact dimensions for vehicular and special forces use, and the MG36, which is actually a heavy-barrelled light support weapon. Several European countries including Germany, Spain and Norway are considering adopting the G36 as a standard weapon, and by most accounts it is an excellent, accurate weapon. In common with most Heckler & Koch products, it is likely to see widespread service.

SPECIFICATIONS

COUNTRY OF ORIGIN: Germany
CALIBRE: 5.56 x 45mm NATO
LENGTH: 999mm (39.33in) stock extended; 758mm (29.84in) stock folded
WEIGHT: 3.4kg (7.49lb)
BARREL: 480mm (18.89in), 6 grooves, rh
FEED: 30-round detachable box magazine
OPERATION: gas
MUZZLE VELOCITY: not available
EFFECTIVE RANGE: not available
CYCLIC RATE OF FIRE: 750rpm

INSAS Assault Rifle

This his indigenous Indian weapon from the Indian Small Arms Factory at Kanpur has given Indian troops a thoroughly modern assault rifle through a process of adapting existing designs to Indian production. The three most seminal assault rifle series of the 20th century – the AK, the M16 and the Heckler & Koch – are present in various elements of the gun and combine to make a reliable, capable gas-operated rifle. Unlike many of these other weapon series, the INSAS is not capable of fully automatic fire – only single shots or three-round burst options are available. This shows a maturity and combat-mindedness on the part of the designers, as fully automatic fire can simply allow the user to empty his rifle inaccurately during a firefight, whereas more limiting types of fire seem to encourage accurate aim by the weapon's users.

SPECIFICATIONS
COUNTRY OF ORIGIN: India
CALIBRE: 5.56 x 45mm NATO
LENGTH: 990mm (38.97in)
WEIGHT: 3.2kg (7.05lb)
BARREL: 464mm (18.26in)
FEED: 20- or 30-round detachable box magazine
OPERATION: gas, self-loading
MUZZLE VELOCITY: 985mps (2903fps)
EFFECTIVE RANGE: 800m (2624ft)
CYCLIC RATE OF FIRE: semi-automatic

SAR 21

The futuristic-looking SAR 21 was adopted by Singapore's armed forces from the late 1990s, accounts of the weapon since then suggesting that it is a high-quality and well-liked piece of kit. A quick glance at the gun reveals a bullpup arrangement, the plastic 30-round box magazine sitting behind the trigger. Internally it is a familiar gas-operating, rotating-bolt weapon, but much of the external gun is made from high-impact polymer, making it a very tough rifle. The carrying handle incorporates an integral 1.5 x magnification telescopic sight, although this handle can be removed and replaced with a Picatinny scope rail for fitting a variety of other sighting devices. The gun can also take an assortment of other accessories, including an underbarrel grenade launcher and an assault-type foregrip. Modular in design, it can also be disassembled into its major assemblies without the need for special tools.

SPECIFICATIONS

COUNTRY OF ORIGIN: Singapore
CALIBRE: 5.56 x 45mm NATO
LENGTH: 805mm (31.69in)
WEIGHT: 3.82kg (8.42lb)
BARREL: 508mm (20in)
FEED: 30-round detachable box magazine
OPERATION: gas
MUZZLE VELOCITY: 970mps (3182fps)
EFFECTIVE RANGE: 800m (2624ft)
CYCLIC RATE OF FIRE: 450–650rpm

IMI Tavor TAR 21

Although the Israel Defense Forces (IDF) have been well-served by rifles such as the M16 and Galil, a replacement rifle was developed in the 1990s by Israel Military Industries (IMI) and named the Tavor TAR 21. The Tavor has since been adopted into Israeli service, although many legacy weapons remain. In basic structure, the TAR 21 is a gas-operated bullpup rifle fitted – like many similar weapons – with an optical sight as standard. It takes the principle of modularity to new levels, however. It can be fitted with the M203 grenade launcher and grenade-launching sight; used with a bipod to create the STAR 21 (designated marksman) rifle; it is also produced in a more compact CTAR assault version. There is even a micro version, the MTAR, which can be converted to 9mm ammunition.

SPECIFICATIONS

COUNTRY OF ORIGIN: Israel
CALIBRE: 5.56 x 45mm NATO
LENGTH: 720mm (28.35in)
WEIGHT: 3.27kg (7.21lb)
BARREL: 460mm (18.11in)
FEED: 30-round detachable box magazine
OPERATION: gas
MUZZLE VELOCITY: 910mps (2986fps)
EFFECTIVE RANGE: 550m (1804ft)
CYCLIC RATE OF FIRE: 750–900rpm

SMALL ARMS 1950–PRESENT SEMI-AUTO AND AUTOMATIC RIFLES

Accuracy International AS50

S ince the 1990s, .50 BMG (12.7 x 99mm) sniper rifles have become increasingly popular as long-range anti-materiel/personnel weapons. The AS50 is a semi-auto rifle in this calibre produced in the UK by the Accuracy International company. It is gas-operated, the massive recoil being controlled by the sheer size of the gun, heavy buffer springs and a sizeable muzzle brake. (The bolt-action version of this rifle, the AW50, has a higher recoil impact.) The magazine holds five rounds and the rifle comes with a folding bipod and rear support leg as standard. Disassembly has been made a simple affair, taking less than three minutes and not requiring special tools. Allied to an appropriate sight, the AS50 can deliver accurate shots to and exceeding 1500m (4921ft), and those struck by the bullet are unlikely to survive the experience.

SPECIFICATIONS
COUNTRY OF ORIGIN: United Kingdom
CALIBRE: 12.7 x 99mm (.50 BMG)
LENGTH: 1369mm (53.89in)
WEIGHT: 14.1kg (31lb)
BARREL: 692mm (27.24in)
FEED: 5-round box magazine
OPERATION: gas
MUZZLE VELOCITY: c. 843mps (2800fps)
EFFECTIVE RANGE: 1500m (4921ft) plus
CYCLIC RATE OF FIRE: n/a

FX-05 Xiuhcoatl

This home-grown Mexican rifle is a recent addition to the list of modern assault rifles. Developed in 2005–06, it was adopted by the Mexican armed forces as an alternative to the Heckler & Koch G36, which was in turn intended to be a replacement for the venerable H&K G3. The Xiuhcoatl – the name means 'Fire Serpent' –is a gas-operated weapon capable of firing either single shot, three-round burst or full auto, the latter at a rate of 750rpm. Weighing 3.9kg (8.59lb), it is nearly 1kg (2.2lb) lighter than the G3, although the fact that it fires the 5.56 x 45mm NATO round rather than the G3's 7.62 x 51mm NATO provides a natural weight advantage. It comes with a Picatinny rail for fitting various scopes and other attachments, has a folding stock, and there are also short-barrelled versions for police and security forces use.

SPECIFICATIONS

COUNTRY OF ORIGIN: Mexico
CALIBRE: 5.56 x 45mm NATO
LENGTH: 1087mm (42.79in)
WEIGHT: 3.9kg (8.59lb)
BARREL: n/a
FEED: 30-round detachable box magazine
OPERATION: gas
MUZZLE VELOCITY: c. 910mps (2986fps)
EFFECTIVE RANGE: 550m (1804ft)
CYCLIC RATE OF FIRE: 750rpm

M110 SASS

The M110 SASS is a new generation of 7.62 x 51mm NATO sniper rifle, developed on the basis of a semi-automatic, gas-operated, rotating-bolt design. Fed from 10- or 20-round box magazines, the semi-auto capability offers the shooter defensive firepower when necessary, but the long-range accuracy is delivered by a heavy freefloating barrel. It is capable of putting a group of shots within 28mm (1.10in) at 91.4m (300ft), and reports back from combat testing in Afghanistan have been extremely positive. Standard fitment on the rifle includes a folding bipod, a collapsible buttstock and the XM151 3.5–10 x variable scope on the MIL-STD-1913 rail system. The barrel also has the option of fitting with a suppressor. Relatively light for a sniper rifle at 7kg (15.43lb), the M110 was voted the #2 best product of 2007 by the US Army.

SPECIFICATIONS

COUNTRY OF ORIGIN: United States
CALIBRE: 7.62 x 51mm NATO
LENGTH: 1028mm (40.47in)
WEIGHT: 7kg (15.43lb)
BARREL: 508mm (20in)
FEED: 10- or 20-round detachable box magazine
OPERATION: gas
MUZZLE VELOCITY: 784mps (2571fps)
EFFECTIVE RANGE: 800m (2624ft)
CYCLIC RATE OF FIRE: not applicable

SMALL ARMS 1950–PRESENT SEMI-AUTO AND AUTOMATIC RIFLES

M39

The M39 is a replacement for the Designated Marksman Rifle (DMR) in US Marine Corps service. Although it has a technologically advanced appearance, its ancestry in the M14 rifle is still evident. It is intended for use by Marine marksmen, soldiers specially trained to take shots out to and beyond 800m (2624ft). The M49 fires the 7.62 x 51mm NATO round (although of match-grade M118LR 175- grain Long Range variety), and is a gas-operated, rotating-bolt design fed from a 20-round box magazine. Its semi-auto capability may not give the accuracy of some bolt-action designs, but it provides the reassurance of back-up firepower if an engagement moves to close quarters. Standard features of the M39 include a variable-length stock, adjustable comb (cheek-piece), a MIL-STD-1913 Picatinny rail for the mounting of scopes and other aiming devices, and a Harris folding bipod.

SPECIFICATIONS

COUNTRY OF ORIGIN: United States
CALIBRE: 7.62 x 51mm NATO
LENGTH: 1123mm (44.21in)
WEIGHT: 7.5kg (16.53lb)
BARREL: 559mm (22in)
FEED: 20-round detachable box magazine
OPERATION: gas
MUZZLE VELOCITY: 863mps (2832fps)
EFFECTIVE RANGE: 800m (2624ft)
CYCLIC RATE OF FIRE: not applicable

FN SCAR

The FN SCAR was designed by FN USA to meet the US Army's requirement for a new Special Operations Forces assault rifle. (The acronym stands for SOF Combat Assault Rifle.) With deliveries beginning in 2005, the SCAR is a typical high-quality FN firearm, and constitutes a completely new design rather than a redevelopment of an existing model. SCAR is a modular series rather than a single weapon. The core of the rifles remains a gas-operated, rotating-bolt system that uses a short-stroke piston movement for efficient weapon cycling. The stock is adjustable for comb height and length of pull, and the guns can take various optical sights or rely on folding, adjustable iron sights. The weapon configuration changes according to what barrel is fitted: free-floating hammer-forged barrels in 254, 356 and 457mm (10, 14 and 18in) lengths are available, each fitted with a three-pronged flash suppressor.

SPECIFICATIONS

COUNTRY OF ORIGIN: United States
CALIBRE: 5.56 x 45mm NATO
LENGTH: 737–990mm (29.02–38.98in)
WEIGHT: 3.5kg (7.72lb)
BARREL: 457mm (17.99in)
FEED: 30-round detachable box magazine
OPERATION: gas
MUZZLE VELOCITY: c. 910mps (2986fps)
EFFECTIVE RANGE: c. 600m (1969ft)
CYCLIC RATE OF FIRE: 600pm

Samopal CZ Model 25

The CZ Model 25 is part of a group of four weapons that began life with the M48A in 1948 (renamed the CZ 23 in 1950). The four weapons are effectively the same except that the CZ 25 has a folding metal stock instead of the wooden stock of the CZ 23, while the CZ 24 and CZ 26 took over from the CZ 23 and CZ 25 in Czech Army service in 1951, these latter guns firing the more powerful 7.62mm Soviet pistol cartridge. Common to all is a distinctive wrapround bolt mechanism: the bolt has a tubular configuration and encloses the rear of the barrel at firing, and the magazine is seated in the pistol-grip itself. Both features contributed to the shortness of the weapon and its general good performance kept it in Czech service until the mid-1960s and, in terrorist hands, to the present day.

SPECIFICATIONS

COUNTRY OF ORIGIN: Czechoslovakia
CALIBRE: 9mm Parabellum
LENGTH: 686mm (27in) stock extended; 445mm (17.52in) stock folded
WEIGHT: 3kg (6.75lb)
BARREL: 284mm (11.18in), 6 grooves, rh
FEED: 24- or 40-round box magazine
OPERATION: blowback
MUZZLE VELOCITY: 395mps (1300fps)
EFFECTIVE RANGE: 120m (394ft)
CYCLIC RATE OF FIRE: 600rpm

Sterling L2A1

The Sterling's signature curved 34-round magazine, 50-year plus service record and its use by more than 90 nations have made it one of the most famous firearms of the twentieth century. It first entered service in the British Army in 1953 as the Sterling L2A1, with the L2A2 and L2A3 appearing in 1953 and 1956, respectively. The Sterling is a resilient and hard-working gun. Its recoil was kept under control by an advanced primer ignition system that actually fired the round a fraction of a second before the round seated itself in the chamber, the breech block then being carried backwards by the leftover force. The Sterling became a standard issue submachine gun across the world and is still made under licence in India, although Sterling ceased trading in 1988.

SPECIFICATIONS

COUNTRY OF ORIGIN: United Kingdom
CALIBRE: 9mm Parabellum
LENGTH: 690mm (27.16in) stock extended; 483mm (19.02in) stock folded
WEIGHT: 2.72kg (5.99lb)
BARREL: 198mm (7.79in), 6 grooves, rh
FEED: 34-round detachable box magazine
OPERATION: blowback
MUZZLE VELOCITY: 395mps (1295fps)
EFFECTIVE RANGE: 70m (230ft)
CYCLIC RATE OF FIRE: 550rpm

Vigneron

There is little exceptional about the Belgian Vigneron submachine gun, though its appearance is slightly unusual on account of the long ribbed barrel, which is fitted with a compensator and muzzle brake. It was a child of the 1950s, constructed from a simple and economical metal-stamping method and made initially for the Belgian Army, seeing active service in the Belgian Congo in the 1960s and subsequently throughout Africa in the hands of various armies once the Belgians had departed. The Vigneron features a pistol grip with an integral safety lever. An unusual feature is its ability to deliver single shots with only a partial pull of the trigger. Its wire stock can also be adjusted to suit the personal dimensions of the user.

SPECIFICATIONS

COUNTRY OF ORIGIN: Belgium
CALIBRE: 9 x 19mm Parabellum
LENGTH: 890mm (35.04in) stock extended; 705mm (27.75in) stock folded
WEIGHT: 3.29kg (7.25lb)
BARREL: 305mm (12in), 6 grooves, rh
FEED: 32-round detachable box magazine
OPERATION: blowback
MUZZLE VELOCITY: 365mps (1200fps)
EFFECTIVE RANGE: 200m (656ft) plus
CYCLIC RATE OF FIRE: 550rpm

Uzi

Beloved of Hollywood thrillers, few weapons have entered into the popular vocabulary or global service as much as the Uzi. It was designed by the talented Lieutenant Uziel Gal in the early years of Israel's existence, when Israel was desperate for a native-produced submachine gun. Gal based his design around the wrapround bolt system found in the Czech vz 23 series, in which the bolt is actually placed forward of the chamber on firing, thus saving a great deal of space and allowing for a longer barrel. Gal's design was an intense success. Simply made and operated, the Uzi is easily held and packs a potent rate of fire. It initally came with a wooden stock, but now a folding metal stock is standard. Used by more than 26 countries outside of Israel, the Uzi has made a definite impact on twentieth-century weapons development.

SPECIFICATIONS

COUNTRY OF ORIGIN: Israel
CALIBRE: 9mm Parabellum
LENGTH: 650mm (25.59in) stock extended; 470mm (18.50in) stock folded
WEIGHT: 3.7kg (8.15lb)
BARREL: 260mm (10.23in), 4 grooves, rh
FEED: 25- or 32-round box magazine
OPERATION: blowback
MUZZLE VELOCITY: 400mps (1312fps)
EFFECTIVE RANGE: 120m (394ft)
CYCLIC RATE OF FIRE: 600rpm

Erma MP58

In the aftermath of World War II, Erma and Walther became two of East and West Germany's most important arms manufacturers, the former producing a new range of submachine guns. The MP58 followed closely on the heels of the MP56, a wraparound-bolt weapon that had few achievements. The MP58 was produced to a Federal Government brief for an economical SMG, and Erma attempted to fulfil this by making most of the MP58 out of single-sheet steel stampings. Unfortunately, the MP58 was turned down for government adoption, despite the gun being essentially well made and reliable (on account of the telescopic mainspring design used during the war). Erma produced several more improved guns, but by the mid-1960s they turned away from military to commercial weapons.

SPECIFICATIONS

COUNTRY OF ORIGIN: Germany
CALIBRE: 9 x 19mm Parabellum
LENGTH: 405mm (15.94in)
WEIGHT: 3.1kg (6.83lb)
BARREL: 190mm (7.48in)
FEED: 30-round detachable box magazine
OPERATION: blowback
MUZZLE VELOCITY: 395mps (1295fps)
EFFECTIVE RANGE: 70m (230ft)
CYCLIC RATE OF FIRE: 650rpm

Samopal 62 Skorpion

This incredibly compact weapon was designed to give tank and vehicle crews (who have little storage space) more advanced firepower than that provided by a mere pistol. Only 270mm (10.63in) long, the Skorpion was capable of putting out 850rpm. More would be possible were it not for a clever restraint on the blowback system in the form of a weight, which is driven down into the grip onto a spring while the bolt is held by a catch; the weight is then pushed up by the spring, disengages the catch and the bolt is released. The Model 61 was the original in 1963 and several variations have appeared since then, some chambered for different calibre rounds. The Skorpion is a terrifying gun at close-quarters owing to its spray effect and it has become an easily concealed firearm of many terrorists worldwide.

SPECIFICATIONS

COUNTRY OF ORIGIN: Czechoslovakia
CALIBRE: 7.65mm (.32 ACP)
LENGTH: 270mm (10.63in)
WEIGHT: 1.31kg (2.87lb)
BARREL: 115mm (4.52in), 6 grooves, rh
FEED: 10 or 20-round detachable box magazine
OPERATION: blowback
MUZZLE VELOCITY: 700rpm
EFFECTIVE RANGE: 50m (164ft)
CYCLIC RATE OF FIRE: 850rpm

Beretta Model 12

A Domenico Salza design, the Model 12 emerged in the mid-1950s. Although Beretta now increased the use of metal stampings to reduce cost, overall quality of the weapon was still retained, this time applied to the tubular receiver design. The Model 12's operation was an orthodox blowback, with the use of a 'wraparound' bolt to reduce the gun length. The receiver was larger than normal to accommodate the bolt that surrounded the barrel, and had two plastic pistol grips at either end, with the magazine in between. The fire selector was a push-through type, and there were two safeties: one conventional, and one below the trigger guard. Accurate and incredibly hardy, the Model 12 found most use with Italian Special Forces and also in the Middle East, Africa and South America, with licensed production in Brazil and Saudi Arabia.

SPECIFICATIONS

COUNTRY OF ORIGIN: Italy
CALIBRE: 9mm Parabellum
LENGTH: 660mm (25.98in) wooden stock; 645mm (25.39in) metal stock extended; 416mm (16.37in) metal stock folded
WEIGHT: 2.95kg (6.50lb)
BARREL: 203mm (7.99in), 6 grooves, rh
FEED: 20-, 30- or 40-round box magazine
OPERATION: blowback
MUZZLE VELOCITY: 380mps (1247fps)
EFFECTIVE RANGE: 120m (394ft)
CYCLIC RATE OF FIRE: 550rpm

Steyr MPi 69

The Steyr MPi 69 is a well-conceived, solid submachine gun that stayed in production between 1969 and 1980. Compact, and with a 550rpm rate of fire, the MPi 69 is a blowback weapon with the unusual feature of fire selection being performed by the trigger pull; pull it half-way back for single shots, and all the way back for full automatic fire. The MPi 69 needs to be distinguished from a later model, the MPi 81. The MPi 69 has the sling attached to the cocking handle, whereas the MPi 81 has a conventional sling attachment and a greater rate of fire (700rpm). The MPi 69's excellent strong construction – the barrel is cold hammered for endurance – has made it a popular export weapon, and it still serves with the Austrian Army in various capacities.

SPECIFICATIONS

COUNTRY OF ORIGIN: Austria
CALIBRE: 9 x 19mm Parabellum
LENGTH: 670mm (26.38in) stock extended; 465mm (18.31in) stock folded
WEIGHT: 3.13kg (6.90lb)
BARREL: 260mm (10.23in), 6 grooves, rh
FEED: 25- or 32-round detachable box magazine
OPERATION: blowback
MUZZLE VELOCITY: 380mps (1247fps)
EFFECTIVE RANGE: 200m (656ft)
CYCLIC RATE OF FIRE: 550rpm

Heckler & Koch MP5

The Heckler & Koch MP5 is a masterpiece of weapons engineering. Its roller-locked delayed blowback system harks back to the German MG42 machine gun and is the same system as the one used in Heckler & Koch's assault rifles. It also fires from a closed chamber, which is part of the reason for its considerable accuracy. The MP5 has now been in production since 1965, although the latest guns have the full range of fire-selection options: single-shot, three-round burst and full automatic. The quality of its machining is consistently excellent and much of the weapon's furniture is plastic to lighten the weapon. There are many variants of the MP5, but the two basic models are the MP5A2, which has a solid plastic butt, and the MP5A3, which has a folding metal stock.

SPECIFICATIONS

COUNTRY OF ORIGIN: Germany
CALIBRE: 9mm Parabellum
LENGTH: 680mm (26.77in)
WEIGHT: 2.55kg (5.62lb)
BARREL: 225mm (8.85in), 6 grooves, rh
FEED: 15- or 30-round detachable box magazine
OPERATION: delayed blowback
MUZZLE VELOCITY: 400mps (1312fps)
EFFECTIVE RANGE: 70m (230ft)
CYCLIC RATE OF FIRE: 800rpm

Sterling L34A1

Development of a silenced version of the Sterling L2 began as far back as 1956, with both Patchett and the Royal Armaments Research & Development Establishment (RARDE) producing prototypes. The latter went through to acceptance and became the Sterling L34A1. The integral suppressor is very effective; the barrel has 72 radial holes drilled into it and is surrounded by a metal cylinder containing baffles into which the firing gases expand and swirl. As with all silencers, muzzle velocity is substantially reduced, but this does not compromise the L34A1 as an effective weapon. Indeed, with recoil lessened, the bolt and recoil spring were lightened, thus making the weapon much more manageable on full-auto than its non-silenced counterpart. Used mainly by special forces soldiers, the L34A1 provides a practical silenced weapon, which promises good performance.

SPECIFICATIONS
COUNTRY OF ORIGIN: United Kingdom
CALIBRE: 9mm Parabellum
LENGTH: 864mm (34.02in) stock extended; 660mm (25.98in) stock folded
WEIGHT: 3.6kg (7.94lb)
BARREL: 198mm (7.79in), 6 grooves, rh
FEED: 34-round detachable box magazine
OPERATION: blowback
MUZZLE VELOCITY: 300mps (984fps)
EFFECTIVE RANGE: 120m (394ft)
CYCLIC RATE OF FIRE: 515rpm

Colt Commando

Quite simply a shorter and lighter version of the M16 assault rifle, the XM177E2 Commando was designed specifically for those units who would value a more compact and lighter weapon in the field, which still retained a high rate of fire and a powerful cartridge. Everything about the Commando – apart from its size – is almost identical to the M16; the parts are interchangeable and it can still be fitted with the M203 grenade launcher if required. The abbreviated dimensions have naturally made it popular with such groups as the US and worldwide special forces and security units because it is easily concealed (its commercial model is known as the Model 733). Further improvements to the rear sights enable the Commando to be used at ranges similar to those of its full-sized brother.

SPECIFICATIONS

COUNTRY OF ORIGIN: United States
CALIBRE: 5.56mm NATO
LENGTH: 808mm (31.81in) stock extended; 552mm (21.73in) stock folded
WEIGHT: 2.5kg (5.51lb)
BARREL: 368mm (14.49in), 6 grooves, rh
FEED: 20- or 30-round box magazine
OPERATION: gas-operated, self-loading
MUZZLE VELOCITY: 830mps (2720fps)
EFFECTIVE RANGE: 400m (1312ft)
CYCLIC RATE OF FIRE: 700–1000rpm

Ingram M10

The Ingram M10's notoriety relies on its brief, concealable dimensions and its astonishingly high rate of fire of over 1000rpm. Despite this combination, the gun is surprisingly controllable, due in the main to its quality workmanship and good balance centred on the pistol grip/magazine receiver. Its designer, Gordon B. Ingram, designed the M10 from 1965–1967 in .45 ACP, although it became more commonly chambered for the 9mm Parabellum. It was originally intended to use the bulbous Sionics Company suppressor (the gun was designated the M11 in this form and used the subsonic .380 (9mm Short) calibre round), which reduced noise almost to just that of the oscillating bolt. With or without the suppressor, the M10 spread across the world amongst covert forces, special police agencies and many criminal elements.

SPECIFICATIONS

COUNTRY OF ORIGIN: United States
CALIBRE: .45 ACP or 9mm Parabellum
LENGTH: 548mm (21.57in) stock extended; 269mm (10.59in) stock folded
WEIGHT: 2.84kg (6.25lb)
BARREL: 146mm (5.75in), 6 grooves, rh
FEED: 32-round box magazine
OPERATION: blowback
MUZZLE VELOCITY: 366mps (1200fps)
EFFECTIVE RANGE: 70m (230ft)
CYCLIC RATE OF FIRE: 1145rpm

Star Z70B

Initially the most notable feature of the Z70B submachine gun was its trigger unit, a case of 1960s design innovation over-reaching itself. In its original form, the Z62, the trigger was in two horizontal sections; pull the top section and you get automatic fire, pull the bottom section and single shots are issued. The design seemed good on paper but was unreliable. It was therefore discarded and changed to a conventional trigger unit, the gun now designated as the Z70B. The Z70B was in most other respects a normal blowback submachine gun made from metal pressings and plastic. However, in terms of operation, it was unusual in that a hammer was used to fire the rounds, controlled by the action of the bolt. The Z70B modification also brought in improved safety features.

SPECIFICATIONS

COUNTRY OF ORIGIN: Spain
CALIBRE: 9 x 19mm Parabellum
LENGTH: 700mm (27.56in) stock extended; 480mm (18.9in) stock folded
WEIGHT: 2.87kg (6.33lb)
BARREL: 200mm (7.87in), 6 grooves, rh
FEED: 20-, 30- or 40-round detachable box magazine
OPERATION: blowback
MUZZLE VELOCITY: 380mps (1247fps)
EFFECTIVE RANGE: 50m (164ft) plus
CYCLIC RATE OF FIRE: 550rpm

Heckler & Koch MP5K

The Heckler & Koch MP5K is a specially compressed version of the MP5, designed for those military or police units who need firepower that can be easily concealed until deployment. Such are its dimensions – only 325mm (12.79in) long – that it can be fitted into a briefcase, carried in a car glove compartment or held under a jacket. Its small size is achieved by the absence of a stock; instead, a front grip is provided for control. Its rate of fire is increased from that of the standard MP5 and reaches 900rpm, the high rpm giving it formidable close-range capabilities. Its compactness tends to see it only fitted with the 15-round magazine, though the 30-round magazines are perfectly useable. Four versions of the MP5K are made, including one, the MP5KA5, which has a three-round burst facility.

SPECIFICATIONS

COUNTRY OF ORIGIN: Germany
CALIBRE: 9mm Parabellum
LENGTH: 325mm (12.79in)
WEIGHT: 2.1kg (4.63lb)
BARREL: 115mm (4.53in), 6 grooves, rh
FEED: 15- or 30-round detachable box magazine
OPERATION: delayed blowback
MUZZLE VELOCITY: 375mps (1230fps)
EFFECTIVE RANGE: 70m (230ft)
CYCLIC RATE OF FIRE: 900rpm

Heckler & Koch MP5SD

The popularity of the Heckler & Koch MP5 series with special forces troops meant that a silenced version, known as the MP5SD, was inevitable. The 9mm Parabellum round it fires is standard and the gun's configuration is little different from any other MP5 model. Yet the integral silencer is particularly effective. The barrel of the MP5SD has 30 x 3mm holes drilled along its length and is surrounded by a two-chamber suppressor, which sequentially diffuses the gases until the round leaves the muzzle at subsonic speed. Both noise and blast reduction are considerable and accuracy remains good over the reduced range. Several varieties of the MP5SD are available, each offering different configurations of furniture, fire-selection (SD 4, 5 and 6 have three-round burst facility) and sight fittings.

SPECIFICATIONS

COUNTRY OF ORIGIN: Germany
CALIBRE: 9mm Parabellum
LENGTH: 550mm (21.65in)
WEIGHT: 2.9kg (6.39lb)
BARREL: 146mm (5.75in), 6 grooves, rh
FEED: 15- or 30-round detachable box magazine
OPERATION: delayed blowback
MUZZLE VELOCITY: 285mps (935fps)
EFFECTIVE RANGE: 50m (164ft)
CYCLIC RATE OF FIRE: 800rpm

Mini-Uzi

Small as the standard Uzi is in itself, the designers at Israel Military Industries have reduced it in scale not once, but twice. The mid-sized Uzi is known as the Mini-Uzi (the smallest is the Micro-Uzi) and its differences from the full-size weapon are limited almost entirely to matters of scale. Having said this, the scaling down of some components has led to a lighter bolt system, which in turn has upped the rate of fire from 600rpm to 950rpm. This firepower can have horrifying effects at close-quarters and the Mini-Uzi has not only become prized by security organizations the world over, but also by many terrorist and criminal elements. Easily concealed, the Mini-Uzi has a special 20-round magazine (although it can accept the full-size magazines) and a single-strut stock that can be used as a foregrip when in the folded position.

SPECIFICATIONS

COUNTRY OF ORIGIN: Israel
CALIBRE: 9mm Parabellum
LENGTH: 600mm (23.62in) stock extended; 360mm (14.17in) stock folded
WEIGHT: 2.7kg (5.95lb)
BARREL: 197mm (7.76in), 4 grooves, rh
FEED: 20-, 25- or 32-round box magazine
OPERATION: blowback
MUZZLE VELOCITY: 352mps (1155fps)
EFFECTIVE RANGE: 50m (164ft)
CYCLIC RATE OF FIRE: 950rpm

Spectre

Apart from its appearance, the Spectre has two unique features that make it ideal for the counter-terrorist and special forces useage for which it was originally designed in the 1980s. The first is that it has a double-action trigger, thus allowing the operator to fire the gun even when it is not cocked just by a pull of the trigger alone; which is a useful facility in the fluid conditions of counter-terrorist operations, where situations can change rapidly requiring instant intervention. The second is its 50-round box magazine, which uses a four-column stacking system to maximise the box capacity (30-round magazines are also used). Such qualities have taken the Spectre into use by several international security forces and should ensure its future for many years to come.

SPECIFICATIONS
COUNTRY OF ORIGIN: Italy
CALIBRE: 9mm Parabellum
LENGTH: 580mm (22.83in) stock extended; 350mm (13.78in) stock folded
WEIGHT: 2.9kg (6.39lb)
BARREL: 130mm (5.12in), 6 grooves, rh
FEED: 30- or 50-round detachable box magazine
OPERATION: blowback
MUZZLE VELOCITY: 400mps (1312fps)
EFFECTIVE RANGE: 50m (164ft)
CYCLIC RATE OF FIRE: 850rpm

BXP

The BXP is an excellent weapon for security and special forces use. It was designed in the early 1980s and produced from 1988, being simply a blowback, wraparound-bolt submachine gun based around the pistol grip/magazine receiver configuration. Where the BXP excels is in overall quality. It is extremely well-balanced and can be fired one-handed when the stock is folded forward, though in this case the stock becomes a solid foregrip. It is made mostly from stainless steel and the rust-resistant coating applied extensively doubles as a dry lubricant. The distinctive muzzle of the BXP can accept a compensator, silencer or even rifle grenade and its overall accuracy is excellent owing to a barrel length of some 208mm (8.18in).

SPECIFICATIONS

COUNTRY OF ORIGIN: South Africa
CALIBRE: 9 x 19mm Parabellum
LENGTH: 607mm (23.89in) stock extended; 387mm (15.24in) stock folded
WEIGHT: 2.5kg (5.51lb)
BARREL: 208mm (8.18in), 6 grooves, rh
FEED: 22- or 32-round detachable box magazine
OPERATION: blowback
MUZZLE VELOCITY: 370mps (1214fps)
EFFECTIVE RANGE: 80m (262ft) plus
CYCLIC RATE OF FIRE: 1000rpm

FN P90

The P90 represents perhaps the future of the submachine gun. Its amorphous design houses unique features throughout. The clear plastic magazine lies across the top of the weapon, with the bullets at a right angle to the barrel, passing through a turntable before being loaded into the chamber. An optical sight is balanced by open sights on both sides for left- or right-handed shooting, and all the gun's operating systems are ambidextrous. Only 400mm (15.75in) long, the P-90 has a receiver that acts as a stock and cartridge ejection is down through the hollow pistol grip. Despite these innovations, the mechanism remains simple blowback, but the cartridge is a new high-power 5.7mm FN, which gives excellent range and penetration. The future popularity and use of such a weapon are yet to be seen.

SPECIFICATIONS

COUNTRY OF ORIGIN: Belgium
CALIBRE: 5.7mm FN
LENGTH: 400mm (15.75in)
WEIGHT: 2.8kg (6.17lb)
BARREL: 263mm (7.75in), 6 grooves, rh
FEED: 50-round detachable box magazine
OPERATION: blowback
MUZZLE VELOCITY: 850mps (2800fps)
EFFECTIVE RANGE: 200m (656ft) plus
CYCLIC RATE OF FIRE: 800–1000rpm

RPD

The RPD may have some hints of the Kalashnikov design in its appearance, but it is actually a Degtyarev weapon. Its abbreviation stands for Ruchnoy Pulemyot Dagtyareva and it became the standard light machine gun in the Soviet forces and those of the satellite communist states from the 1950s to the mid-1970s. The RPD had an average capability. It fired M1943 cartridges – the first Soviet machine gun to fire the intermediate round – from a drum-contained belt-feed mechanism that tended to be unreliable in dirty conditions. The RPD was strictly a light machine gun; it had no removable barrel, so fire had to be controlled and generally kept below 100rpm. Steady improvements over its 20-year service made the RPD a good squad support weapon and one that still features in the developing world.

SPECIFICATIONS

COUNTRY OF ORIGIN: Soviet Union/Russia
CALIBRE: 7.62 x 39mm M1943
LENGTH: 1041mm (40.98in)
WEIGHT: 7kg (15.43lb)
BARREL: 520mm (20.47in), 4 grooves, rh
FEED: 100-round belt
OPERATION: gas, air-cooled
MUZZLE VELOCITY: 735mps (2410fps)
EFFECTIVE RANGE: 900m (2953ft)
CYCLIC RATE OF FIRE: 700rpm

AAT-52

The Arme Automatique Transformable (AAT-52) was produced from 1952 and became the French Army's standard general-purpose machine gun. A rather ungainly-looking weapon, it works on a delayed blowback operation that has a two-part bolt and a lighter front section, which receives the initial impetus of recoil and forces through a delay lever to push back a heavy rear section and open the breech. The AAT-52 has some good features, not least its ability to switch between light and heavy barrels for support- and sustained-fire roles, respectively. The latter role has a purpose-designed tripod, as opposed to the standard bipod, which is attached to the barrel, a real inconvenience for barrel changes. The AAT-52 was later converted to the 7.62mm NATO round and was labelled the AAT-52/mle NF-1.

SPECIFICATIONS

COUNTRY OF ORIGIN: France
CALIBRE: 7.5 x 54mm M1929/7.62 x 51mm NATO
LENGTH: 990mm (38.97in) stock retracted; 1145mm (45.07in) stock extended
WEIGHT: 9.9kg (21.75lb)
BARREL: 500mm (19.68in), 4 grooves, rh; heavy barrel 600mm (23.62in)
FEED: 50-round, disintegrating-link belt
OPERATION: delayed blowback, air-cooled
MUZZLE VELOCITY: 840mps (2755fps)
EFFECTIVE RANGE: 1000m (3280ft)
CYCLIC RATE OF FIRE: 475rpm

NF-1

The AAT-52 was a perfectly good weapon in all respects and served French forces well. However, its 7.5 x 54mm cartridge set it at odds with NATO standardisation to the 7.62mm round, so old machine guns have been recalibrated and new ones made to conform with NATO specifications. In this format it is know as the NF-1. It comes in light- and heavy-barrelled versions, but, in both cases, the switch to the 7.62 x 51mm NATO cartridge has resulted in a marked improvement in performance – the NF-1 has increased the AAT-52's effective range by 200–400m (656–1312ft). Yet some problems remain, especially the difficult barrel change arrangement in which the bipod comes off with the barrel and thus gives the operator no support while holding the hot gun.

SPECIFICATIONS

COUNTRY OF ORIGIN: France
CALIBRE: 7.62 x 51mm NATO
LENGTH: 1245mm (49.02in)
WEIGHT: 11.37kg (25.07lb)
BARREL: 600mm (23.62in), 4 grooves, rh
FEED: disintegrating-link belt
OPERATION: delayed blowback
MUZZLE VELOCITY: 830mps (2723fps)
EFFECTIVE RANGE: 1200m (3937ft) plus
CYCLIC RATE OF FIRE: 900rpm

M60

Despite being the dominant US Army GPMG from Vietnam to the Gulf War, the M60's history is full of problems. Developed in the late 1950s, it was an amalgam of Germany's MG42 and FG42 respectively. Despite this, and features such as the Stellite linings on the barrels that allow firing even when the barrel is white hot, the M60 was plagued by deficiencies. Barrel change was awkward as there was no handle and each barrel had its own cylinder and bipod. Thus the firer had to wrestle with the red-hot barrel using an asbestos glove (easily lost during combat). The M60E1 had its own barrel handle and kept the bipod and gas-cylinder separate, however, gas-operation was prone to fouling and jamming (leading soldiers in Vietnam to call it 'the Pig'). Despite its inefficiencies, the M60 stayed in widespread service for several decades, but is now being phased out.

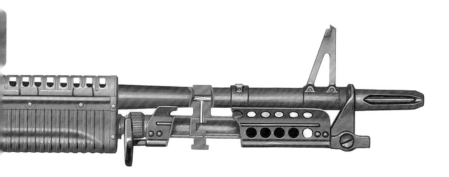

SPECIFICATIONS

COUNTRY OF ORIGIN: United States
CALIBRE: 7.62mm NATO
LENGTH: 1110mm (43.75in)
WEIGHT: 10.4kg (22.93lb)
BARREL: 560mm (22.05in), 4 grooves, rh

FEED: disintegrating-link belt
OPERATION: gas, air-cooled
MUZZLE VELOCITY: 855mps (2805fps)
EFFECTIVE RANGE: 3000m (9843ft) plus
CYCLIC RATE OF FIRE: 600rpm

FN MAG

The unquestionable talents of Belgium's Fabrique Nationale Herstal are seldom more apparent than in the FN MAG (Mitrailleur à Gaz), one of the twentieth century's seminal machine guns. The FN MAG perfected the concept of the general-purpose machine gun (GPMG). To adapt to different roles, a gas regulator control allows the operator to vary the gas pressure drawn from the barrel and thus alter the rate of fire. The barrel is quickly changed in combat and the whole weapon is stocky and robust, giving it a reliability that has transported it across the world. The weapon feeds from the left-hand side from open-link, metal ammunition belts. US Army tests showed that the FN MAG is able to fire an average of 26,000 rounds between failures under battlefield conditions, making it one of the most reliable GPMGs in existence. This also explains why it has remained in service in armies throughout the world for more than 50 years in various guises.

SPECIFICATIONS

COUNTRY OF ORIGIN: Belgium
CALIBRE: 7.62 x 51mm NATO
LENGTH: 1250mm (49.21in)
WEIGHT: 10.15kg (22.25lb)
BARREL: 546mm (21.49in), 4 grooves, rh
FEED: metal-link belt, various lengths
OPERATION: gas, air-cooled
MUZZLE VELOCITY: 853mps (2800fps)
EFFECTIVE RANGE: 3000m (9843ft)
CYCLIC RATE OF FIRE: 600–1000rpm

MG42/59

The MG42 emerged in 1941 from Germany's need to speed up machine gun manufacture over that of the superb, but expensive, MG34. Therefore, Mauser looked to new production methods such as those used for the MP40 submachine gun. Production and output of the MG42 was dramatically increased by using metal stamping and welding instead of machining. In addition, a superb new locking system was introduced, using two locking rollers which cammed outwards to recesses on the receiver walls, and a quick-change barrel facility made the gun very popular with users. The result was a light, accurate, functional machine gun with a very high rate of fire. It first appeared in Africa and Russia in 1942 and soon became a source of fear for Allied troops. A variant of the MG42, the MG45, was curtailed by the end of World War II.

SPECIFICATIONS

COUNTRY OF ORIGIN: Germany
CALIBRE: 7.92 x 57mm Mauser
LENGTH: 1220mm (48.03in)
WEIGHT: 11.5kg (25.35lb)
BARREL: 535mm (21.07in), 4 grooves, rh
FEED: 50-round belt
OPERATION: short recoil, air-cooled
MUZZLE VELOCITY: 800mps (2650fps)
EFFECTIVE RANGE: 3000m (9843ft) plus
CYCLIC RATE OF FIRE: 1200rpm

L7A2

Made by Belgian arms producer Fabrique Nationale, the FN MAG was first designed in the 1950s by M. Ernest Vervier and has been used or made under license in more than 80 countries since. The weapon's name is an abbreviation for Mitrailleuse d'Appui Général, meaning general purpose machine gun (GPMG). In Britain, it is made under licence as the L7A1 and later the L7A2; more than 80 other countries have also taken it into their forces. The L7 was adopted by the British Army as a replacement for the long-serving Vickers machine gun and the Bren, following trials in 1957. The FN MAG can be mounted on both its own front bipod for the light support roles or a heavy tripod for sustained fire deployments. It was this reliability that influenced the US Army into deciding to develop the MAG as their M240 series GPMG, replacing the M60 machine gun.

SPECIFICATIONS

COUNTRY OF ORIGIN: Belgium
CALIBRE: 7.62mm x 51mm NATO
LENGTH: 1263mm (49.72in)
WEIGHT: 10.85kg (23.92lb)
BARREL: 543mm (21.38in)
FEED: metal-link belt, various lengths
OPERATION: gas, air-cooled
MUZZLE VELOCITY: 853mps (2800fps)
EFFECTIVE RANGE: 800m (2624ft)
CYCLIC RATE OF FIRE: 650–1000rpm

7.62mm Maschinengewehr 3

The 7.62mm Maschinengewehr 3 (MG3) is instantly recognizable as a derivative of the revered MG42. During the 1950s, the German Army assessed international weaponry for its rearmament and found that the MG42 was yet to be surpassed. Thus the MG1 was produced, almost identical in every way to the MG42, with fractional changes to feed mechanism and bolt. An evolving chain of upgrades and modifications ensued (in particular, the shift to the 7.62mm NATO rounds), leading to the current MG3, the standard light machine gun used by the German forces and many other armies around the world. The MG3 retains the original MG42's high rate of fire, although this can be varied with the use of the V550 bolt or the heavier V950 bolt. The feed can equally accept German DM1 and DM13 belts and US M13 belts.

SPECIFICATIONS

COUNTRY OF ORIGIN: Germany
CALIBRE: 7.62 x 51mm NATO
LENGTH: 1220mm (48.03in)
WEIGHT: 11.5kg (25.35lb)
BARREL: 531mm (20.91in), 4 grooves, rh
FEED: belt feed
OPERATION: short recoil, air-cooled
MUZZLE VELOCITY: 820mps (2690fps)
EFFECTIVE RANGE: 3000m (9843ft) plus
CYCLIC RATE OF FIRE: 1300rpm (V550 bolt); 950rpm (V950 bolt)

PKM 7.62mm

The PK established the general-purpose machine gun within the ranks of the Soviet Army and its variations equip Russian and many other armies around the world to this day. The gun is simplicity itself, being based on the Kalashnikov rotary-bolt system and having very few internal parts. Those parts work well, however, whether used in light-support or sustained-fire roles. The PK's one oddity is its use of the old M91 (1891) rimmed cartridge, which can generate some feed problems, but does outreach the M1943 round. The PK series is extensive, but each version is mainly distinguished by mountings. The PKM is rather different, in that the weight of the barrel is reduced and there is a greater use of stampings. It and later models can be visually separated from the others by their unfluted barrel.

SPECIFICATIONS
COUNTRY OF ORIGIN: Soviet Union/Russia
CALIBRE: 7.62 x 39mm M1943
LENGTH: 1160mm (45.67in)
WEIGHT: 9kg (19.84lb)
BARREL: 658mm (25.91in), 4 grooves, rh
FEED: 100-, 200- or 250-round belt
OPERATION: gas, air-cooled
MUZZLE VELOCITY: 800mps (2600fps)
EFFECTIVE RANGE: 2000m (6562ft) plus
CYCLIC RATE OF FIRE: 710rpm

Heckler & Koch HK21

Essentially a belt-feed, heavy-barrelled version of the ubiquitous G3 rifle, the HK21 maintained the rifle's general excellence in quality and fire capability. It fulfilled all the criteria for a general-purpose machine gun: light, with a good rate of suppressive fire (900rpm) and an effective range of around 2000m (6562ft). These qualities took it from German service to use by Portugal (where it is now manufactured under licence), Africa and Southeast Asia. As part of the Heckler & Koch range, it was easy to modify the HK21 for G3 magazine feed and it could also accept 5.56 x 45mm or 7.62 x 39mm rounds with changes of the barrel, belt-feed plate and bolt. The HK21 was followed by two subsequent designs: the HK21A1 (which had the magazine option removed and faster belt loading) and the HK21E.

SPECIFICATIONS

COUNTRY OF ORIGIN: Germany
CALIBRE: 7.62 x 51mm NATO
LENGTH: 1021mm (40.19in)
WEIGHT: 7.92kg (17.46lb)
BARREL: 450mm (17.72in), 4 grooves, rh
FEED: belt feed
OPERATION: delayed blowback, air-cooled
MUZZLE VELOCITY: 800mps (2625fps)
EFFECTIVE RANGE: 2000m (6562ft)
CYCLIC RATE OF FIRE: 900rpm

RPK

The RPK is quite simply a standard AKM assault rifle fitted with a longer, heavier barrel and a bipod. It was introduced as the replacement for the RPD machine gun and its identical operating method to the AKM meant that any soldier familiar with this weapon could fire the RPK without any additional training (at least in the mechanics of its firing). In some senses, however, directly scaling up the assault rifle has caused problems. The fixed barrel means that the rpm needs to be kept to below 75 to avoid overheating, although the chromium-plating on bore and barrel make these components hard wearing. The RPK can accept any AKM magazines, but also takes a 40-round box or a 75-round drum. The more recent RPK-74 is the light support version of the AK-74 rifle, both in 5.54mm calibre.

SPECIFICATIONS
COUNTRY OF ORIGIN: Soviet Union/Russia
CALIBRE: 7.62 x 39mm M1943
LENGTH: 1041mm (40.98in)
WEIGHT: 4.76kg (10.49lb)
BARREL: 589mm (23.2in), 4 grooves, rh
FEED: 30- or 40-round box or 75-round drum
OPERATION: gas, air-cooled
MUZZLE VELOCITY: 732mps (2400fps)
EFFECTIVE RANGE: 800m (2624ft)
CYCLIC RATE OF FIRE: 600rpm

Minigun M134

The M134 Minigun sits at the far edge of the category 'small arms', as it was only intended for mounted use in helicopters. Its rotating six-barrelled configuration harks back to Gatling's famous machine gun, but in this case power is supplied by an electric motor. The result is a rate of fire that can reach up to 6000rpm. This awesome firepower was brought into action specifically for the Vietnam War. Here the Minigun was clamped either into helicopter door positions or in special gun pods, and they were used for spraying the jungle floor with 7.62mm slugs. Each barrel has its own bolt unit and the feed is from a 4000-round belt which is usually stored in a drum. For sheer fire-to-size ratio, the Mingun takes some beating. It has made a number of appearances in Hollywood films.

SPECIFICATIONS

COUNTRY OF ORIGIN: United States
CALIBRE: 7.62 x 51mm NATO
LENGTH: 800mm (31.49in)
WEIGHT: 15.9kg (35.05lb)
BARREL: 559mm (22in), 4 grooves, rh
FEED: 4000-round link belt feed
OPERATION: electrically powered revolver
MUZZLE VELOCITY: 869mps (2850fps)
EFFECTIVE RANGE: 3000m (9843ft) plus
CYCLIC RATE OF FIRE: up to 6000rpm

Stoner 63 Light Machine Gun

The light machine gun within the Stoner system was designed to give soldiers a sustained-fire capability, while the box-contained 150-round belt feed enabled the soldier to wield the weapon like a heavy assault rifle. It had a quick-change barrel facility in which the barrel was removed by the carrying handle and was generally fitted with either a single foregrip or a bipod. The major difference between the light machine gun and the standard Stoner was that the receiver was inverted to place the ejection port on the left of the gun, with the gas system now located below the barrel. All Stoner 63 weapons had a gas-adjustment control situated in the front sight block. This allowed the firer to control the rpm while also limiting fouling when using varieties of ammunition.

SPECIFICATIONS

COUNTRY OF ORIGIN: United States
CALIBRE: 5.56 x 45mm NATO
LENGTH: variable; short barrel, no butt stock 660mm (25.98in)
WEIGHT: variable; around 4.9kg (10.80lb)
BARREL: long 551mm (21.69in); short 397mm (15.6in)
FEED: 20-round magazine to 150-round belt
OPERATION: gas, air-cooled
MUZZLE VELOCITY: 1000mps (3300fps)
EFFECTIVE RANGE: 1000m (3280ft)
CYCLIC RATE OF FIRE: 700–1000rpm

Stoner 63 Medium Machine Gun

Little differentiates the Stoner medium machine gun from its lighter version, except that it is capable of being mounted on a M2 tripod through the use of an adaptor. Once mounted in this way, it is a good onboard weapon for vehicular or helicopter use. The one consequence of the mounting is that the gun must be used with an open belt feed, rather than boxed feed, although a few boxed carries are suitable. Since its original appearance, the Stoner machine gun has been through fairly turbulent times, exiting and entering production according to its own performance limits and military politics. The latest version from Knight's Armament Company, Florida, is lighter and more reliable than its predecessors and is designed to break down into only six components when field stripped.

SPECIFICATIONS

COUNTRY OF ORIGIN: United States
CALIBRE: 5.56 x 45mm NATO
LENGTH: variable; short barrel, no butt stock 660mm (25.98in)
WEIGHT: variable; around 4.9kg (10.80lb)
BARREL: long 551mm (21.69in); short 397mm (15.6in)
FEED: 20-round magazine to 150-round belt
OPERATION: gas, air-cooled
MUZZLE VELOCITY: 1000mps (3300fps)
EFFECTIVE RANGE: 1000m (3280ft)
CYCLIC RATE OF FIRE: 700–1000rpm

Stoner M63 Machine Gun

The Stoner M63 machine gun is actually a weapons system, rather than an individual gun. It was developed by Eugene Stoner in the early 1960s, based on the idea of having a standard receiver onto which different configurations of barrels, stocks and feed systems could be fitted. The result was six weapon options out of a single mechanism: carbine, light machine gun, automatic rifle, medium machine gun, mounted machine gun for vehicular use, and commando configuration (introduced later in 1969). The Stoner was a revolutionary proposition, and elite units such as the US Navy SEALs used it in Vietnam, generally with a 150-round belt box feed system. The Stoner has suffered from reliability problems, however, mainly due to its susceptibility to dirt and a weak ejector.

SPECIFICATIONS

COUNTRY OF ORIGIN: United States
CALIBRE: 5.56 x 45mm NATO
LENGTH: variable; short barrel, no butt stock 660mm (25.98in)
WEIGHT: variable; around 4.9kg (10.80lb)
BARREL: long 551mm (21.69in); short 397mm (15.6in)
FEED: 20-round magazine to 150-round belt
OPERATION: gas, air-cooled
MUZZLE VELOCITY: 1000mps (3300fps)
EFFECTIVE RANGE: 1000m (3280ft)
CYCLIC RATE OF FIRE: 700–1000rpm

XM-214

The XM-214 never reached beyond the prototype stage. It followed the six-barrelled, externally powered configuration of weapons like the Minigun, but used the smaller 5.56mm round that is now NATO standard. If anything, the Six-Pak, as it was affectionately know, was even more versatile in its fire suppression role than its 7.62mm predecessors. It was capable of complete control over rate of fire, as the user could select from 1000, 2000, 3000, 4000 or 6000rpm or alter the speed of barrel rotation to achieve anything between 400 and 10,000rpm. Such high rates of fire may well be the reason that the XM-214 attracted no orders, as the logistical demands of keeping such a fast-firing weapon fed with rounds were problematic. Actual feed was from two 500-round cassettes on either side of the gun.

SPECIFICATIONS

COUNTRY OF ORIGIN: United States
CALIBRE: 5.56 x 45mm NATO
LENGTH: 685mm (26.98in)
WEIGHT: 38.6kg (85.09lb), including 1000 rounds
BARREL: 455mm (17.91in), 4 grooves, rh
FEED: belt fed from two 500-round cassettes
OPERATION: electrically powered revolver
MUZZLE VELOCITY: 990mps (3250fps)
EFFECTIVE RANGE: 2000m (6562ft) plus
CYCLIC RATE OF FIRE: 400–10,000rpm

M240

The Belgian FN MAG was, and remains, one of the most successful machine guns of the post-World War II era. Hence it was no surprise that the US armed forces adopted the weapon from the late 1970s, largely to replace the troubled M60 as a general-purpose machine gun. Relabelled the M240, it was first applied as a coaxial tank gun, but during the 1980s its use spread into other vehicular and infantry applications. As with the FN MAG, it is a 7.62 x 51mm NATO belt-fed, gas-operated weapon. Its rate of fire can be adjusted from a low (650rpm) setting to a high (950rpm) setting. There are several US variants, which include the M240C, a right-side-feed gun for use on the Bradley M2/M3 or Marine Corps Light Armored Vehicle (LAV), and the M240D, configured for use aboard helicopters.

SPECIFICATIONS

COUNTRY OF ORIGIN: Belgium/USA
CALIBRE: 7.62 x 51mm NATO
LENGTH: 1260mm (49.61in)
WEIGHT: 13kg (28.66lb) on bipod
BARREL: 545mm (21.46in)
FEED: disintegrating belt
OPERATION: gas
MUZZLE VELOCITY: 650 or 950rpm
EFFECTIVE RANGE: 1000m (3280ft) plus
CYCLIC RATE OF FIRE: 650 or 950rpm

Heckler & Koch HK21E

Heckler & Koch's continual development of its HK21 range of machine guns has now arrived at the HK21E series. The appearance is little changed from the standard HK21, but the receiver has been lengthened to create a more manageable recoil, adding an extra 119mm (4.69in) to the overall length. As with the HK21, the HK21E can take both belt and magazine feed through simple adaptation of the bolt mechanism; in the case of the HK21E, firing options have been extended to include a three-round burst in addition to single shot and full automatic. Further improvements in the HK21E are drum-type rear sights (which work better with the lengthened receiver) and the fitting of front grips to allow firing from the hip in assault manoeuvres.

SPECIFICATIONS

COUNTRY OF ORIGIN: Germany
CALIBRE: 7.62 x 51mm NATO
LENGTH: 1140mm (44.88in)
WEIGHT: 9.3kg (20.50lb)
BARREL: 560mm (22.04in), 4 grooves, rh
FEED: belt feed, variable belt length
OPERATION: gas, air-cooled
MUZZLE VELOCITY: 840mps (2755fps)
EFFECTIVE RANGE: 1000m (3280ft) plus
CYCLIC RATE OF FIRE: 800rpm

CETME Ameli

CETME were already renowned for
their rifles when they introduced the
Ameli in 1982. Its visual heritage in the
German MG42 is deceptive, as the Ameli
uses the roller-locked delayed blowback
system it has applied in its Model L
rifle, and some parts are interchangeable
between the two weapons. This system
makes it both reliable and fast firing,
reaching up to 1200rpm, though the gun
can easily be modified to reduce its rate
of fire to 850rpm. The Ameli now comes
in two versions: a standard weapon and
a lightweight version, which is over 1kg
(2.2lb) lighter through its production
in lighter alloys. Though currently only
used by Spain and Mexico, the Ameli is
a superb gun and should achieve more
widespread international use.

SPECIFICATIONS

COUNTRY OF ORIGIN: Spain
CALIBRE: 5.56 x 45mm NATO
LENGTH: 970mm (38.19in)
WEIGHT: 6.35kg (13.99lb) standard; 5.2kg (11.46lb)
lightweight
BARREL: 400mm (15.75in), 6 grooves, rh
FEED: 100- or 200-round boxed belt
OPERATION: gas-operated, air cooled
MUZZLE VELOCITY: 875mps (2870fps)
EFFECTIVE RANGE: 1000m (3280ft) plus
CYCLIC RATE OF FIRE: 850 or 1200rpm

FN Minimi

The FN Minimi is a superb example of a light squad automatic weapon developed specifically for using the 5.56mm NATO round. It emerged from the FN factories in the early 1970s and its keynotes were reliability – it uses a roller-guided locking system, which is extremely smooth and uncomplicated – and its ability to switch between belt feed and magazine feed (using the standard M16 magazines) without adjustment. These features, and others such as a feed indicator (showing the number of rounds left in the magazine) and detachable trigger guard for gloved/NBC use, have bought it a place in many armies including the US Army, where it is known as the M249 Squad Automatic Weapon. FN also make a short barrel and telescoping stock version for special unit use.

SPECIFICATIONS

COUNTRY OF ORIGIN: Belgium
CALIBRE: 5.56 x 45mm NATO
LENGTH: 1040mm (40.94in)
WEIGHT: 6.83kg (15.05lb)
BARREL: 466mm (18.34in), 6 grooves, rh
FEED: 100- or 200-round belt or 30-round magazine
OPERATION: gas, air-cooled
MUZZLE VELOCITY: 915mps (3000fps)
EFFECTIVE RANGE: 2000m (6562ft) plus
CYCLIC RATE OF FIRE: 750–1100rpm

M249

The M249 Squad Automatic Weapon (SAW) is largely the Belgian Minimi machine gun, but renamed and slightly modified for US production and service. It was adopted by the US Army in 1982, although manufacture did not actually begin until the early 1990s. In terms of US modifications, most involve minor internal changes to suit US manufacturing processes, although the US gun is also fitted with a perforated steel heat shield

above the barrel. (This limits optical distortion from heat waves rising off the barrel.) The M249 was acquired to provide base-of-fire capability for four-man infantry squads. In this role, it has more than proved itself in Afghanistan and Iraq, reliably delivering 5.56mm (0.22in) fire at a cyclical rate of 750rpm. Like the Minimi, it can feed from standard M16 magazines as well as the more typical boxed 200-round belt.

SPECIFICATIONS

COUNTRY OF ORIGIN: Belgium/United States
CALIBRE: 5.56 x 45mm NATO
LENGTH: 1040mm (40.94in)
WEIGHT: 6.85kg (15.10lb)
BARREL: 523mm (20.59in)

FEED: 30-round box magazine or 200-round belt
OPERATION: gas
MUZZLE VELOCITY: 915mps (3000fps)
EFFECTIVE RANGE: 1000m (3280ft)
CYCLIC RATE OF FIRE: 750rpm

M60E3

At 10.5kg (23.15lb), the standard M60 machine gun was a little too heavy for some light machine gun roles, so a lightweight version was produced and designated as the M60E3. The distinguishing feature of the M60E3 is the forward pistol grip that makes firing from the hip perfectly possible; however, as the gun still weighs 8.61kg (18.98lb), this act requires formidable upper body and arm strength. Other features that separate the M60E3 from its parent are a new loading mechanism for the belt and a lightweight bipod. The M60E3 has not totally overcome some of the deficiencies of its parent, but elite groups such as the US Navy SEALs and the US Marines have found it to their liking and use it in a variety of support roles.

SPECIFICATIONS

COUNTRY OF ORIGIN: United States
CALIBRE: 7.62 x 51mm NATO
LENGTH: 1067mm (42in)
WEIGHT: 8.61kg (18.98lb)
BARREL: 560mm (22.04in), 4 grooves, rh
FEED: disintegrating-link belt feed
OPERATION: gas, air-cooled
MUZZLE VELOCITY: 860mps (2821fps)
EFFECTIVE RANGE: 1100m (3609ft) plus
CYCLIC RATE OF FIRE: 550rpm

IMI Negev

Adopted by the Israel Defense Forces (IDF) in 1988, the home-grown Negev machine gun reflects similar principles of design to the Belgian Minimi. It is a light squad weapon firing 5.56 x 45mm NATO rounds, working from a standard gas-operated mechanism. Like the Minimi, the gas regulator can be adjusted to alter the rate of fire, from 650rpm to 950rpm, and there is even a gas shut-off setting to allow the weapon to fire rifle grenades from the muzzle. The feed system is flexible; it can take box (standard rifle) magazines as well as the belts. One interesting feature is its convertibility. Not only can it change its role by fitting to various mounts, it can also be transformed into a regular assault rifle by removing the bipod and fitting a standard rifle fore-end.

SPECIFICATIONS

COUNTRY OF ORIGIN: Israel
CALIBRE: 5.56 x 45mm NATO
LENGTH: 1020mm (40.16in)
WEIGHT: 7.2kg (15.87lb)
BARREL: 460mm (18.11in)
FEED: 35-round box magazine or 150-round belt
OPERATION: gas
MUZZLE VELOCITY: 950mps (3115fps)
EFFECTIVE RANGE: 1000m (3280ft)
CYCLIC RATE OF FIRE: 650–950rpm

Heckler & Koch MG4

The MG4 is Heckler & Koch's contribution to the 5.56mm light machine gun category, competing against the likes of Fabrique Nationale's Minimi. Like the Minimi, it is a relatively compact 5.56 x 45mm NATO machine gun fed from disintegrating-link belts. (The belts are contained in plastic boxes for ease of movement.) The barrel system is of quick-change variety, and the carrying handle acts as a grip during the barrel change, meaning that the user requires no special protective glove. The MG4 comes with an integral bipod, although the gun can be fitted to a variety of other mounts, and the stock can be folded down for packing or more convenient battlefield movement; the gun is fireable even while the stock is folded. The receiver feedtray cover can take a Picatinny rail for fitting various other sights.

SPECIFICATIONS

COUNTRY OF ORIGIN: Germany
CALIBRE: 5.56 x 45mm NATO
LENGTH: 1030mm (40.55in) stock extended
WEIGHT: 8.2kg (18.07lb)
BARREL: 460mm (18.11in)
FEED: 30-round detachable box magazine
OPERATION: gas
MUZZLE VELOCITY: 910mps (2986fps)
EFFECTIVE RANGE: 550m (1804ft)
CYCLIC RATE OF FIRE: 750–900rpm

M79 Grenade Launcher

The M79 was a breech-loading single-shot grenade launcher, which became a familiar weapon during the Vietnam conflict. It fired a 40mm grenade to a range of about 400m (1312ft) and, when loaded with high explosive, had an impressive kill radius of more than 5m (16ft). A variety of shells could be fired from the M79, including buckshot, flechette, airburst, smoke, flares and CS gas canisters, and the rifled barrel ensured that the M79 had good accuracy over an effective range of around 150m (492ft). The spin produced by the rifling also caused the grenade to arm itself after about 30m (98ft) of flight through a shift in internal weights. Some 350,000 'Bloopers' (as they were known by the troops in Vietnam) were produced between 1961 and 1971, and the M79 can still be found in use across the world today.

SPECIFICATIONS

COUNTRY OF ORIGIN: United States
CALIBRE: 40mm
LENGTH: 783mm (30.83in)
WEIGHT: 2.95kg (6.50lb) loaded
BARREL: not known
FEED: single round
OPERATION: breech-loaded, single shot
MUZZLE VELOCITY: 75mps (245fps)
EFFECTIVE RANGE: 150m (492ft)
CYCLIC RATE OF FIRE: not applicable

AGS-17

The AGS-17 is one of a series of belt-fed automatic grenade launchers that emerged in various world armies from the 1960s onwards. Unlike the similar US 40mm Mark 19, which it resembled, the AGS-17 came in 30mm calibre, although it did also operate on the basis of a blowback action. The recoil forces of this operation were controlled through the mount, and the AGS-17 could be either used as an infantry weapon or operated from a helicopter or vehicle platform. The feed system used on the gun was belt feed, and this enabled the operator to lay down a systematic bombardment on targets to ranges of up to 1200m (3937ft). In this capacity, it was used to lethal effect against the guerrilla fighters in Afghanistan's mountainous terrain during the Soviet occupation of the country in the 1980s.

SPECIFICATIONS

COUNTRY OF ORIGIN: Soviet Union/Russia
CALIBRE: 30mm
LENGTH: 840mm (33.07in)
WEIGHT: 18kg (39.68lb) without tripod
BARREL: not available
FEED: belt feed
OPERATION: blowback, automatic
MUZZLE VELOCITY: not known
EFFECTIVE RANGE: 1200m (3937ft)
CYCLIC RATE OF FIRE: not known

Mk 19 Grenade Launcher

The Mk 19 Grenade Launcher became a popular harassing tool against the Vietcong during the Vietnam War. There it was first mounted onto a number of US river patrol craft used to control the Vietnamese coastline, which could bombard enemy positions ranged along the river bank with a stream of high-explosive 40mm (1.57in) grenades. This proved to be an effective application for the weapon and the Mark 19's customers increased to include the US Army and Israeli forces, with both finding the Mark 19 a useful and deadly weapon when placed on vehicle mountings. A blowback grenade launcher capable of full-automatic fire feeding from a disintegrating link belt-feed, it fires from an open bolt (the bolt stays back from the chamber between firing), which helps the weapon to stay cool when firing repeatedly without pause.

SPECIFICATIONS

COUNTRY OF ORIGIN: United States
CALIBRE: 40mm
LENGTH: 1028mm (40.47in)
WEIGHT: 34kg (74.96lb)
BARREL: not available
FEED: belt feed, disintegrating-link belt
OPERATION: blowback
MUZZLE VELOCITY: 240mps (790fps)
EFFECTIVE RANGE: 1600m (5249ft)
CYCLIC RATE OF FIRE: not applicable

Granatpistole

The Granatpistole comes from the estimable name of Heckler & Koch and is a fairly conventional break-open 40mm (1.57in) grenade launcher. Its primary virtues are its portability and size, as the stock folds down and gives the weapon a convenient 463mm (18.23in) length. The fact that the Granatpistole can also be safely fired in the stock-folded position has added to its overall credibility as a weapon, and it has gone into service successfully with the German army and also with various security and special forces troops. Like most grenade launchers, the Granatpistole can fire a variety of shells, such as high-explosive and tear gas, and its range of about 300m (984ft) means that it has practical applications both for long-range lob shots or flat-trajectory firing at closer ranges. It is likely to remain in service for some time.

SPECIFICATIONS

COUNTRY OF ORIGIN: Germany
CALIBRE: 40mm
LENGTH: 683mm (26.89in) stock extended; 463mm (18.23in) stock folded
WEIGHT: 2.3kg (5.07lb)
BARREL: not available
FEED: single round, breech-loaded
OPERATION: breech-loaded
MUZZLE VELOCITY: 75mps (245fps)
EFFECTIVE RANGE: 300m (984ft)
CYCLIC RATE OF FIRE: not applicable

Brunswick RAW

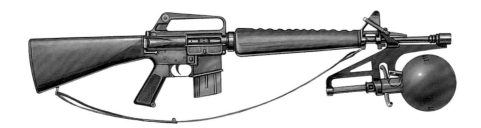

While the M203 grenade launcher has become a common mount on the US M16 rifle, the Brunswick Rifleman's Assault Weapon (RAW) still has some way to go to acceptance. The unusual spherical bomb is fired from the M16 and is intended for use against light vehicles and in urban settings. In flight, the bomb is rocket assisted; when it strikes the target, its contents – 1.27kg (2.79lb) of high explosive – are plastered onto the surface, then detonated (rather like the HESH shell used by tanks). The results are admittedly impressive, as it can blow its way through 200mm (7.87in) of reinforced concrete. The capabilities of the RAW are somewhat lessened by the awkwardness of its shape and attachment. It is undoubtedly useful for short-range urban combat roles and its explosive power is greater than the M203, but whether it will become a regular attachment on the end of rifles remains to be seen.

SPECIFICATIONS

COUNTRY OF ORIGIN: United States
CALIBRE: 140mm
LENGTH: 305mm (12in)
WEIGHT: 3.8kg (8.36lb)
BARREL: not applicable
FEED: single round
OPERATION: rifle fired
MUZZLE VELOCITY: 180mps (590fps)
EFFECTIVE RANGE: 200m (656ft) plus
CYCLIC RATE OF FIRE: not applicable

Remington M870

Remington has had a long history of firearms manufacture in all weapon types, not least shotguns. Its M870 series of guns has been extensively used for police and military work across the world, particularly for riot and close-quarter operations, respectively. Perhaps the defining military model was the M870 Mk 1. This was adopted by the US Marines Corps in the mid-1960s. It was a standard pump-action shotgun that was durable, powerful, had a good magazine capacity (seven rounds) and was decisive in putting a man down at close range. This killing force was tested in anger in Vietnam by Marine and US Navy SEAL teams. It could fire standard shot, flechettes, solid slugs or various other forms of ammunition. The Mk 1 still serves today around the world in assorted roles, alongside a broad family of other M870 weapons.

SPECIFICATIONS

COUNTRY OF ORIGIN: United States
CALIBRE: 12 gauge
LENGTH: 1060mm (41.73in)
WEIGHT: 3.6kg (7.94lb)
BARREL: 533mm (20.98in)
FEED: 7-round integral tubular magazine
OPERATION: pump action
MUZZLE VELOCITY: variable, depending on type of ammunition
EFFECTIVE RANGE: 100m (328ft)
CYCLIC RATE OF FIRE: not applicable

Mossberg ATPS 500

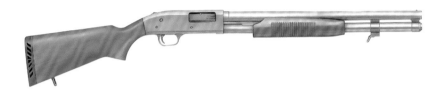

The Mossberg 500 series of shotguns began its life in the 1960s as a new exploration into combat shotguns for the company O.F. Mossberg & Sons Inc. Its current forms include models for hunting, home security and military use, but the ATPS was specifically designed for military applications. The Model 500 is in most senses a conventional pump action shotgun, even if a very robust one. The quality of machining is outstanding and all the internal components are made from very high-grade steel. Special features of the ATPS, which reflect its possible usage in combat, include a bayonet mount and even a telescopic sight mounting for greater accuracy when firing slugs. A new bullpup-type Model 500 known as the Bullpup 12 is also now on the market, but the conventional 500 retains great loyalty among its many users.

SPECIFICATIONS

COUNTRY OF ORIGIN: United States
CALIBRE: 12
LENGTH: 1070mm (42.13in)
WEIGHT: 3.3kg (7.27lb)
BARREL: 510mm (20.08in)
FEED: 6-round integral tubular magazine
OPERATION: pump action
MUZZLE VELOCITY: variable, depending on type of ammunition
EFFECTIVE RANGE: 100m (328ft)
CYCLIC RATE OF FIRE: not applicable

Winchester 12 Defender

Winchester is one of the US's most venerable rifle manufacturers and it produces a high-quality range of shotguns. The Winchester 12 – a 12-gauge pump-action shotgun that entered service in World War II – is still used today for police and military work. The basic specifications of the Winchester 12 include a six- or seven-round under-barrel tubular magazine (the number of rounds carried depends on the type of cartridges), various sight configurations for the firing of shot or slugs, and good-quality finishes to the metalwork, which are either blued, Parkerised or stainless steel (the latter being a particular police version). The Defender Model is the essential Model 12 and current issues can be with a stock in conventional format or without a stock and featuring a pistol grip, these being ideal for security operations where the weapon needs to be concealed until required.

SPECIFICATIONS

COUNTRY OF ORIGIN: United States
CALIBRE: 12 gauge
LENGTH: not available
WEIGHT: 3.06kg (6.74lb), variations apply
BARREL: 457mm (17.99in)
FEED: 6- or 7-round integral tubular magazine
OPERATION: pump action
MUZZLE VELOCITY: variable, depending on type of ammunition
EFFECTIVE RANGE: 200m (656ft)
CYCLIC RATE OF FIRE: not applicable

Franchi SPAS 12

The Franchi SPAS 12 is a purpose-designed combat shotgun and boasts many features that make it eminently versatile in roles from crowd control to military use. It first emerged as the Model 11 in 1979, and the Model 12 followed shortly afterwards with a folding version of the skeleton metal stock, which also featured an arm hook for one-armed firing. Both models are pump action and semi-automatic; the mode is selected by a single button under the fore-end. They can even fire full auto, shooting out everything from bird shot and single slugs to teargas projectiles. Its pattern of spread using a standard 12-gauge cartridge is 0.9m (2ft 11in) to 40m (131ft 2in), making it a fearsome weapon to face. The SPAS Modellos 11 and 12 have revolutionised combat shotgun design, and the black phosphated metal creates a sense of visual threat, which alone has proved useful in action.

SPECIFICATIONS

COUNTRY OF ORIGIN: Italy
CALIBRE: 12
LENGTH: 930mm (36.61in) stock extended; 710mm (27.95in) stock folded
WEIGHT: 4.2kg (9.26lb)
BARREL: 460mm (18.11in)
FEED: 7-round integral tubular magazine
OPERATION: pump action and gas (for semi-auto/full-auto modes)
MUZZLE VELOCITY: variable, depending on type of ammunition
EFFECTIVE RANGE: 100m (328ft)
CYCLIC RATE OF FIRE: 240rpm when on full-auto

Milkor MGL

The South African Milkor MGL is one of a new breed of revolver-type grenade launchers designed for roles ranging from hand-held riot-control applications to airborne and vehicle use in combat. Its semi-automatic operation allows six 40mm grenades to be fired in less than three seconds, giving it impressive firepower, and the ammunition types fired include high explosive, plastic shot, smoke, tear gas and baton rounds (the ammunition types can be mixed in the magazine if required). In combat the MGL's effective range moves from a minimum of 30m (98ft) to a maximum of 400m (1312ft), and accuracy is sustained by the occluded eye gunsight (OEG) featuring a built-in range estimator. The MGL is a gas-operated weapon and is also available in a twin mounted configuration for use on vehicles or on its own tripod fitting.

SPECIFICATIONS

COUNTRY OF ORIGIN: South Africa
CALIBRE: 40mm
LENGTH: 788mm (31.02in) stock extended; 566mm (22.28in) stock folded
WEIGHT: 5.3kg (11.68lb)
BARREL: 310mm (12.20in) 6 grooves, rh
FEED: gas, semi-automatic
OPERATION: 6-round revolving cylinder
MUZZLE VELOCITY: 75mps (245fps)
EFFECTIVE RANGE: 400m (1312ft)
CYCLIC RATE OF FIRE: not applicable

Pancor Jackhammer

The space-age appearance of the Pancor Jackhammer denotes its place amongst a new breed of combat shotguns. It is set in a bullpup configuration with the 10-round 'ammunition cassette' set behind the trigger group. This cassette is a revolver-feed magazine, which, once emptied, is detached and replaced by a new cassette ready to fire. the old cassette is not reloaded, neither is there any ejection of rounds, they are simply retained inside the cassette. Each cassette comes pre-loaded in sealed packaging, which denotes the type of ammunition within. The Jackhammer has a gas-operated system, which, on full-automatic setting, is capable of a cyclic rate of fire of 240rpm. Unlike many other automatic shotguns, the Jackhammer can sustain this fire owing to an effective muzzle compensator and a very rugged construction in steel and high-impact plastics.

SPECIFICATIONS

COUNTRY OF ORIGIN: United States
CALIBRE: 12 gauge
LENGTH: 762mm (30in)
WEIGHT: 4.57kg (10.08lb) loaded
BARREL: 457mm (17.99in)
FEED: 10-round detachable pre-loaded rotary cassette
OPERATION: gas
MUZZLE VELOCITY: variable, depending on type of ammunition
EFFECTIVE RANGE: 200m (656ft) plus
CYCLIC RATE OF FIRE: 240rpm

Benelli M4 Super 90

The Italian Benelli M4 was the winner of a 1990s competition to source a new combat shotgun for the US armed forces, and from 1999 it became a service shotgun in the US Marine Corps. Working on a semi-auto, gas-operated system (it has dual self-cleaning gas pistons for increased reliability), the M4 resembles a traditional shotgun only in its 12-gauge calibre. As well as a variety of camouflage finishes, the gun comes with a drilled and tapped receiver with Picatinny rail as standard. Its basic sight is an M4 Tactical rear ghost ring sight, adjustable for windage and elevation, and a front post, but the rail means the shotgun can take many other optical sights. Magazine capacity of the tubular, under-barrel magazine is eight rounds, plus an additional round in the chamber if so chosen. The stock is collapsible.

SPECIFICATIONS

COUNTRY OF ORIGIN: Italy
CALIBRE: 120-gauge
LENGTH: 1010mm (39.76in) stock extended
WEIGHT: 3.8kg (8.37lb)
BARREL: 470mm (18.50in)
FEED: 8-round tubular magazine
OPERATION: gas
MUZZLE VELOCITY: varies according to cartridge type
EFFECTIVE RANGE: varies according to cartridge type
CYCLIC RATE OF FIRE: not applicable

Franchi SPAS 15

One of the problems of the conventional pump-action shotgun is the time it takes to reload the weapon once all the shells have been emptied from the tubular magazine. After considering this problem, the Franchi concern developed several magazine-loading prototypes, including a bullpup configuration weapon that did not make it into production. There followed the SPAS 14, a magazine-loaded version of the SPAS 12, and then the SPAS 15. In appearance, the SPAS 15 looks much like an assault rifle, with a detachable 10-round magazine and a fire selection facility allowing the user to switch between semi-automatic and pump action. Full automatic was considered by Franchi, but the ergonomic and practical problems of excessive recoil were never overcome, so this is not yet a feature offered by the company's shotguns.

SPECIFICATIONS

COUNTRY OF ORIGIN: Italy
CALIBRE: 12
LENGTH: 980 or 1000mm (38.58 or 39.37in)
WEIGHT: 3.9 or 4.1kg (8.59 or 9.04lb)
BARREL: 450mm (17.71in)
FEED: 10-round detachable box magazine
OPERATION: pump action and gas
MUZZLE VELOCITY: variable, depending on type of ammunition
EFFECTIVE RANGE: 100m (328ft)
CYCLIC RATE OF FIRE: semi-automatic

Index

A

AAT-52 136
Accuracy International AS50 111
Accuracy International L96A1 62
AGS-17 162
AN-94 103
Armalite AR-18 73
Astra Falcon 28

B

Barrett 'Light Fifty' M82A1 96
Benelli M4 Super 90 172
Beretta 93R 48
Beretta AR70/90 79
Beretta BM59 69
Beretta Model 12 122
Beretta Model 81 40
Beretta Model 92SB 47
Beretta SC70 95
Beretta Sniper 63
Brunswick RAW 165
BXP 133

C

Calico M950 51
CETME 67
CETME Ameli 154
Colt Commando 126
Colt Python 26
CZ75 37

D

Dragunov SVD 72

E

Enfield L85A1 (SA80) 97
Erma MP58 120

F

FAMAS 91
FN F2000 102
FN FAL Para 65
FN Five-Seven 55
FN FNC 84
FN MAG 140
FN Minimi 155
FN P90 134
FN SCAR 115
Franchi SPAS 12 169
Franchi SPAS 15 173
FR-F1 59
FX-05 Xiuhcoatl 112

G

Galil ARM 80
Galil Sniper 81
Glock 17 46
Glock 18 49
Glock 20 50
Granatpistole 164

H

Heckler & Koch G11 100
Heckler & Koch G3 75
Heckler & Koch G36 107
Heckler & Koch G3SG1 77
Heckler & Koch HK13E 76

Heckler & Koch HK21 145
Heckler & Koch HK21E 153
Heckler & Koch MG4 160
Heckler & Koch MP5 124
Heckler & Koch MP5K 129
Heckler & Koch MP5SD 130
Heckler & Koch P11 43
Heckler & Koch P7 41
Heckler & Koch P9 31
Heckler & Koch PSG 1 83
Helwan 33

I

IMI Desert Eagle 45
IMI Negev 159
IMI Tavor TAR 21 110
Ingram M10 127
INSAS Assault Rifle 108
Iver Johnson Model 500 64

K

Kalashnikov AK-103 101
Kalashnikov AK-74 87
Kalashnikov AKM 70–71
Kalashnikov AKS-74 88
Kalashnikov AKSU-74 89

L

L1A1 Self-loading Rifle 66
L7A2 142
L85A1 Carbine 98
Light Support Weapon L86A1 99

M

M110 113
M14 68
M16A1 74
M21 Rifle 78
M240 152
M249 156–7
M39 114
M4 104–5
M40A1 56
M60 138–9
M60E3 158
M79 Grenade Launcher 161
MAB PA-15 39
Manurhin MR73 35
Mark 19 Grenade Launcher 163
Maschinengewehr 3, 7.62mm 143
Mauser SP66 60
MBA Gyrojet 13mm 29
MG42/59 141
Milkor MGL 170
Minigun 147
Mini-Uzi 131
Mossberg ATPS 500 167

N

NF-1 137

P

Pancor Jackhammer 171
Parker-Hale Model 85 61
PKM 7.62mm 144
PSM 36

Q

QBZ-95 106

R

Remington M870 166
RPD 135
RPK 146
Ruger Mini-14 82
Ruger Redhawk 44
Ruger Security Six 34

S

Samopal 62 Skorpion 121
Samopal CZ Model 25 116
SAR 21 109
SAR 80 94
SIG SG540 86
SIG-Sauer P-225 38
SIG-Sauer P-226 52
Smith & Wesson 1006 54
Smith & Wesson 459 32
Smith & Wesson Mk 22 30
Smith & Wesson Model 29.44 Magnum 27
Spectre 132
Star 30M 53
Star Z70B 128
Stechkin 25
Sterling L2A1 117
Sterling L34A1 125
Steyr MPi 69 123
Steyr SSG 69 58
Steyr-Mannlicher AUG 90
Stoner 63 Light Machine Gun 148
Stoner 63 Medium Machine Gun 149
Stoner M63 Machine Gun 150

T

Tokagypt 58 24

U

Uzi 119

V

Valmet M76 85
Vektor R4 92
Vigneron 118

W

Walther P5 42
Walther WA2000 93
Weatherby Mk V 57
Winchester 12 Defender 168

X

XM-214 151